MyStatLab™

www.mystatlab.com

MyStatLab is a text-specific, easily customizable online course that integrates interactive multimedia instruction with content from your Pearson textbook. As a part of the MyMathLab® series, MyStatLab courses include all of MyMathLab's standard features, plus additional resources designed specifically to help students succeed in statistics, such as Java™ applets, statistical software, and more.

Features for Instructors

MyStatLab provides you with a rich and flexible set of course materials, along with course-management tools that make it easy to deliver all or a portion of your course online.

Powerful homework and test manager ▶

Create, import, and manage online homework assignments, quizzes, and tests that are automatically graded, allowing you to spend less time grading and more time teaching. You can choose from a wide range of assignment options, including time limits, proctoring, and maximum number of attempts allowed.

◀ Custom exercise builder

The MathXL® Exercise Builder (MEB) for MyStatLab lets you create static and algorithmic online exercises for your online assignments. Exercises can include number lines, graphs, and pie charts, and you can create custom feedback that appears when students enter answers.

Comprehensive gradebook ▶

MyStatLab's online gradebook automatically tracks your students' results on tests, homework, and tutorials. The gradebook provides a number of flexible grading options, including exporting grades to a spreadsheet program such as Microsoft® Excel.

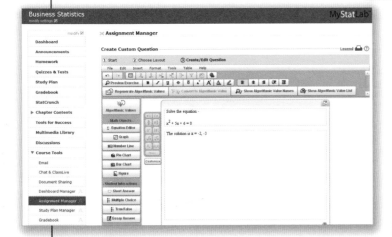

Features for Students

MyStatLab provides students with a personalized, interactive environment where they can learn at their own pace and measure their progress.

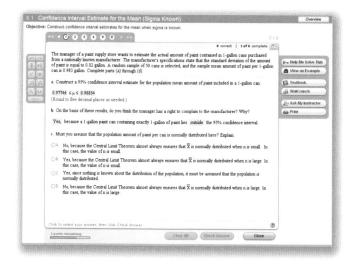

◄ Interactive tutorial exercises

MyStatLab's homework and practice exercises, correlated to the exercises in the textbook, are generated algorithmically, giving students unlimited opportunity for practice and mastery. Exercises include guided solutions, sample problems, and learning aids for extra help at point-of-use, and they offer helpful feedback when students enter incorrect answers.

StatCrunch ►

StatCrunch offers both numerical and data analysis and uses interactive graphics to illustrate the connection between objects selected in a graph and the underlying data. In most MyStatLab courses, all data sets from the textbook are pre-loaded in StatCrunch, and StatCrunch is also available as a tool from all online homework and practice exercises.

Student Purchasing Options

There are many ways for students to sign up for MyStatLab:

- Use the access kit bundled with a new textbook
- Purchase a stand-alone access kit from the bookstore
- Register online through **pearsonmylabandmastering.com**

A ROADMAP FOR SELECTING A STATISTICAL METHOD

Type of Analysis	TYPE OF DATA	
	Numerical	Categorical
Describing a group or several groups	Ordered array, stem-and-leaf display, frequency distribution, relative frequency distribution, percentage distribution, cumulative percentage distribution, histogram, polygon, cumulative percentage polygon (**Sections 2.3, 2.5**) Mean, median, mode, quartiles, range, interquartile range, standard deviation, variance, coefficient of variation, boxplot (**Sections 3.1, 3.2, 3.3**)	Summary table, bar chart, pie chart, Pareto chart (**Sections 2.2, 2.4**)
Inference about one group	Confidence interval estimate of the mean (**Sections 8.1 and 8.2**) t test for the mean (**Section 9.2**)	Confidence interval estimate of the proportion (**Section 8.3**) Z test for the proportion (**Section 9.4**)
Comparing two groups	Tests for the difference in the means of two independent populations (**Section 10.1**) Paired t test (**Section 10.2**) F test for the difference between two variances (**Section 10.4**)	Z test for the difference between two proportions (**Section 10.3**) Chi-square test for the difference between two proportions (**Section 11.1**)
Comparing more than two groups	One-way analysis of variance (**Section 10.5**)	Chi-square test for differences among more than two proportions (**Section 11.2**)
Analyzing the relationship between two variables	Scatter plot, time series plot (**Section 2.6**) Covariance, coefficient of correlation (**Section 3.5**) Simple linear regression (**Chapter 12**) t test of correlation (**Section 12.7**)	Contingency table, side-by-side bar chart, (**Sections 2.2, 2.4**) Chi-square test of independence (**Section 11.3**)
Analyzing the relationship between two or more variables	Multiple regression (**Chapter 13**)	Multidimensional contingency tables (**Section 2.7**)

Business Statistics

A First Course

SIXTH EDITION

Business Statistics

A First Course

SIXTH EDITION

David M. Levine

Department of Statistics and Computer Information Systems

Zicklin School of Business, Baruch College, City University of New York

Timothy C. Krehbiel

Department of Management

Richard T. Farmer School of Business, Miami University

Mark L. Berenson

Department of Management and Information Systems

School of Business, Montclair State University

PEARSON

Boston   Columbus   Indianapolis   New York   San Francisco   Upper Saddle River
Amsterdam   Cape Town   Dubai   London   Madrid   Milan   Munich   Paris   Montreal   Toronto
Delhi   Mexico City   São Paulo   Sydney   Hong Kong   Seoul   Singapore   Taipei   Tokyo

Editorial Director: Sally Yagan
Editor in Chief: Donna Battista
Senior Acquisitions Editor: Chuck Synovec
Editorial Project Manager: Mary Kate Murray
Editorial Assistant: Ashlee Bradbury
Director of Marketing: Maggie Moylan
Executive Marketing Manager: Anne Fahlgren
Senior Managing Editor: Judy Leale
Production Project Manager: Jane Bonnell
Senior Operations Supervisor: Arnold Vila
Operations Specialist: Cathleen Petersen
Creative Director: Blair Brown
Senior Art Director/Supervisor: Janet Slowik

Art Director: Steve Frim
Interior Designers: Dina Curro/Suzanne Behnke
Cover Designer and Art: LCI Design
Associate Media Project Manager, Editorial:
  Sarah Peterson
Media Project Manager, Production: John Cassar
Composition/Full-Service Project Management:
  PreMediaGlobal
Printer/Binder: Courier/Kendallville
Cover Printer: Lehigh-Phoenix
  Color/Hagerstown
Text Font: TimesNewRomanPS
Technical Editor: David Stephan

Credits and acknowledgments borrowed from other sources and reproduced, with permission, in this textbook appear on the appropriate page within text.

Microsoft and/or its respective suppliers make no representations about the suitability of the information contained in the documents and related graphics published as part of the services for any purpose. All such documents and related graphics are provided "as is" without warranty of any kind. Microsoft and/or its respective suppliers hereby disclaim all warranties and conditions with regard to this information, including all warranties and conditions of merchantability, whether express, implied or statutory, fitness for a particular purpose, title and non-infringement. In no event shall Microsoft and/or its respective suppliers be liable for any special, indirect or consequential damages or any damages whatsoever resulting from loss of use, data or profits, whether in an action of contract, negligence or other tortious action, arising out of or in connection with the use or performance of information available from the services.

The documents and related graphics contained herein could include technical inaccuracies or typographical errors. Changes are periodically added to the information herein. Microsoft and/or its respective suppliers may make improvements and/or changes in the product(s) and/or the program(s) described herein at any time. Partial screen shots may be viewed in full within the software version specified.

Microsoft® and Windows® are registered trademarks of the Microsoft Corporation in the U.S.A. and other countries. This book is not sponsored or endorsed by or affiliated with the Microsoft Corporation.

Many of the designations by manufacturers and sellers to distinguish their products are claimed as trademarks. Where those designations appear in this book, and the publisher was aware of a trademark claim, the designations have been printed in initial caps or all caps.

Library of Congress Cataloging-in-Publication Data
Levine, David M.
  Business statistics : a first course / David M. Levine, Timothy C. Krehbiel, Mark L. Berenson.—6th ed.
    p. cm.
  ISBN 978-0-13-280726-5
  1. Commercial statistics.   2. Industrial management—Statistical methods.   I. Krehbiel, Timothy C.
  II. Berenson, Mark L.   III. Title.
  HF1017.B382 2013
  519.5—dc23   2011045734

10 9 8 7 6 5 4 3 2 1

ISBN 10:   0-13-280726-2
ISBN 13: 978-0-13-280726-5

To our wives,
Marilyn L., Patti K., and Rhoda B.

and to our children,
Sharyn, Ed, Rudy, Rhonda, Kathy, and Lori

About the Authors

Photo courtesy of Rudy Krehbiel

The textbook authors meet to discuss statistics at a Mets baseball game. Shown left to right: David Levine, Mark Berenson, and Tim Krehbiel.

David M. Levine is Professor Emeritus of Statistics and Computer Information Systems at Baruch College (City University of New York). He received B.B.A. and M.B.A. degrees in Statistics from City College of New York and a Ph.D. from New York University in Industrial Engineering and Operations Research. He is nationally recognized as a leading innovator in statistics education and is the co-author of 14 books, including such best-selling statistics textbooks as *Statistics for Managers Using Microsoft Excel*, *Basic Business Statistics: Concepts and Applications*, *Business Statistics: A First Course*, and *Applied Statistics for Engineers and Scientists Using Microsoft Excel and Minitab*.

He also is the co-author of *Even You Can Learn Statistics: A Guide for Everyone Who Has Ever Been Afraid of Statistics*, currently in its 2nd edition, *Six Sigma for Green Belts and Champions* and *Design for Six Sigma for Green Belts and Champions*, and the author of *Statistics for Six Sigma Green Belts*, all published by FT Press, a Pearson imprint, and *Quality Management*, 3rd edition, McGraw-Hill/Irwin. He is also the author of *Video Review of Statistics* and *Video Review of Probability*, both published by Video Aided Instruction, and the statistics module of the MBA primer published by Cengage Learning. He has published articles in various journals, including *Psychometrika*, *The American Statistician*, *Communications in Statistics*, *Decision Sciences Journal of Innovative Education*, *Multivariate Behavioral Research*, *Journal of Systems Management*, *Quality Progress*, and *The American Anthropologist*, and given numerous talks at the Decision Sciences Institute (DSI), American Statistical Association (ASA), and Making Statistics More Effective in Schools and Business (MSMESB) conferences. Levine has also received several awards for outstanding teaching and curriculum development from Baruch College.

Timothy C. Krehbiel is Professor of Management and Senior Associate Dean of the Farmer School of Business at Miami University in Oxford, Ohio. He teaches undergraduate and graduate courses in business statistics. In 1996, he received the prestigious Instructional Innovation Award from the Decision Sciences Institute. He has also received the Farmer School of Business Effective Educator Award and has twice been named MBA professor of the year.

Krehbiel's research interests span many areas of business and applied statistics. His work has appeared in numerous journals, including *Quality Management Journal, Ecological Economics, International Journal of Production Research, Journal of Purchasing and Supply Management, Journal of Applied Business Research, Journal of Marketing Management, Communications in Statistics, Decision Sciences Journal of Innovative Education, Journal of Education for Business, Marketing Education Review, Journal of Accounting Education,* and *Teaching Statistics.* He is a co-author of three statistics textbooks published by Prentice Hall: *Business Statistics: A First Course, Basic Business Statistics,* and *Statistics for Managers Using Microsoft Excel.* Krehbiel is also a co-author of the book *Sustainability Perspectives in Business and Resources.*

Krehbiel graduated *summa cum laude* with a B.A. in history from McPherson College and earned an M.S. and a Ph.D. in statistics from the University of Wyoming.

Mark L. Berenson is Professor of Management and Information Systems at
Montclair State University (Montclair, New Jersey) and also Professor Emeritus of Statistics and Computer Information Systems at Bernard M. Baruch College (City University of New York). He currently teaches graduate and undergraduate courses in statistics and in operations management in the School of Business and an undergraduate course in international justice and human rights that he co-developed in the College of Humanities and Social Sciences.

Berenson received a B.A. in economic statistics and an M.B.A. in business statistics from City College of New York and a Ph.D. in business from the City University of New York.

Berenson's research has been published in *Decision Sciences Journal of Innovative Education, Review of Business Research, The American Statistician, Communications in Statistics, Psychometrika, Educational and Psychological Measurement, Journal of Management Sciences and Applied Cybernetics, Research Quarterly, Stats Magazine, The New York Statistician, Journal of Health Administration Education, Journal of Behavioral Medicine,* and *Journal of Surgical Oncology.* His invited articles have appeared in *The Encyclopedia of Measurement & Statistics* and *Encyclopedia of Statistical Sciences.* He is co-author of 11 statistics texts published by Prentice Hall, including *Statistics for Managers Using Microsoft Excel, Basic Business Statistics: Concepts and Applications,* and *Business Statistics: A First Course.*

Over the years, Berenson has received several awards for teaching and for innovative contributions to statistics education. In 2005, he was the first recipient of The Catherine A. Becker Service for Educational Excellence Award at Montclair State University.

Brief Contents

Contents

3 Numerical Descriptive Measures   92

4 Basic Probability   140

5 Discrete Probability Distributions   176

6 The Normal Distribution 200

7 Sampling and Sampling Distributions 226

8 Confidence Interval Estimation 256

9 Fundamentals of Hypothesis Testing: One-Sample Tests   294

10 Two-Sample Tests and One-Way ANOVA   334

11 Chi-Square Tests 402

12 Simple Linear Regression 430

13 Multiple Regression   486

🌐 Online Chapter:
14 Statistical Applications in Quality Management

Appendices 523

Preface

Educational Philosophy

Seeking ways to continuously improve the teaching of business statistics is the core value that guides our works. We actively participate in Decision Sciences Institute (DSI), American Statistical Association (ASA), and Making Statistics More Effective in Schools and Business (MSMESB) conferences. We use the Guidelines for Assessment and Instruction (GAISE) reports as well as our reflections on teaching business statistics to a diverse student body at several large universities. These experiences have helped us identify the following key principles:

1. **Show students the relevance of statistics**   Students need a frame of reference when learning statistics, especially when statistics is not their major. That frame of reference for business students should be the functional areas of business, such as accounting, finance, information systems, management, and marketing. Each statistics topic needs to be presented in an applied context related to at least one of these functional areas. The focus in teaching each topic should be on its application in business, the interpretation of results, the evaluation of the assumptions, and the discussion of what should be done if the assumptions are violated.

2. **Familiarize students with the statistical applications used in the business world** Integrating these programs into all aspects of an introductory statistics course allows the course to focus on interpretation of results instead of computations. Introductory business statistics courses should recognize that programs with statistical functions are commonly found on a business decision maker's desktop computer, therefore making the *interpretation* of results more important than the tedious hand calculations required to produce them.

3. **Provide clear instructions to students for using statistical applications**   Books should explain clearly how to use programs such as Excel and Minitab with the study of statistics, without having those instructions dominate the book or distract from the learning of statistical concepts.

4. **Give students ample practice in understanding how to apply statistics to business**   Both classroom examples and homework exercises should involve actual or realistic data as much as possible. Students should work with data sets, both small and large, and be encouraged to look beyond the statistical analysis of data to the interpretation of results in a managerial context.

New to This Edition: Enhanced Statistical Coverage

This 6th edition of *Business Statistics: A First Course* builds on previous editions with these new and enhanced features:

- The use of the DCOVA (**D**efine, **C**ollect, **O**rganize, **V**isualize, and **A**nalyze) framework as an integrated approach for applying statistics to help solve business problems.
- Many new applied examples and exercises, with data from *The Wall Street Journal*, *USA Today*, and other sources.
- "Managing Ashland MultiComm Services," a new integrated case that appears at the ends of chapters throughout the book (replacing the *Springville Herald* case).
- "Digital Cases," interactive PDF files that create a new series of cases that appear at the ends of chapters throughout the book (replacing the Web Cases).
- An expanded discussion of using Excel and Minitab to summarize and explore multidimensional data.
- Revised and updated "Think About This" essays (formerly entitled "From the Author's Desktop") that provide greater insight into what has just been learned and raise important issues about the application of statistical knowledge.
- Additional in-chapter Excel and Minitab results.

New to This Edition: Expanded Excel and Minitab Guides

In this 6th edition of *Business Statistics*: *A First Course*, the instructions for using Excel and Minitab have been revised, reorganized, and enhanced in new end-of-chapter guides and back-of-the book appendices. These sections support students by:

- Providing a readiness checklist and orientation that guide students through the process of getting ready to use Excel or Minitab (see Chapter 1 and the Chapter 1 Excel and Minitab Guides).
- Incorporating Excel Guide workbooks that serve as models and templates for using Excel for statistical problem solving. These free and reusable workbooks, annotated examples of which appear throughout the chapters of this book, can be used by students in their other courses or in their jobs.
- Allowing students to use Excel with or without PHStat2 and with or without the Analysis ToolPak (an Excel component that is not available in Mac Excel 2008).
- Expanding the scope of Minitab Guide instructions.
- Reviewing common operations, such as opening, saving, and printing results (see Chapter 1 Excel and Minitab Guides).
- Explaining the different types of files available online that support this book and how to download those files (Appendix C).
- Providing a separate appendix that discusses software configuration issues, including how to check for Excel and Minitab updates and how to configure Excel for use with PHStat2 or the Analysis ToolPak (Appendix D).
- An appendix that discusses formatting and other intermediate-level Excel operations (Appendix F).
- Answering frequently asked questions about Excel, PHStat2, the Pearson statistical add-in for Microsoft Windows–based Excel versions, and Minitab (the new Appendix G).
- In Appendix Section C.4, offering a complete list of all downloadable files for this book. (See "Student Resources" on page xxii for more details about the files and programs that can be downloaded.)

Chapter-by-Chapter Changes in the 6th Edition

The 6th edition features Excel and Minitab Guides at the end of each chapter that replace the software appendices of the previous edition. Organized by in-chapter subsections for easy cross-reference, these new guides contain an expanded discussion of how to apply Excel and Minitab to the statistical methods discussed in a chapter. The Excel Guides present instructions for using Excel without employing an add-in (*In-Depth Excel*); instructions for using PHStat2, the add-in that allows students to focus on the results that Excel creates; and, when appropriate, instructions for using the Analysis ToolPak, the Microsoft Office add-in that is included in most versions of Excel. The Minitab Guides have been greatly expanded to better match the scope of the material covered by the Excel Guides.

The 6th edition also contains a number of other global changes. End-of-chapter Digital Cases that use interactive PDF documents update and replace the Web Cases. A new integrated case, "Managing Ashland MultiComm Services," replaces the "Managing the *Springville Herald*" case in Chapters 2, 3, 5, 6, 7, and 9 through 13. End-of-chapter summaries and roadmaps have been enhanced in selected chapters. And Appendices B through D and F and G have been revised and reorganized to provide enhanced help for students seeking answers to questions about using the software and online resources for this book. Highlights of the changes to the individual chapters are as follows:

Chapter 1 Sections 1.1 and 1.2 have been rewritten to focus on the increasing role of statistics in business. The 5th edition's Section 1.5 has been moved to Chapter 2. Section 1.4 has been rewritten and retitled "How to Use This Book" and now includes the "Checklist for Getting Started" (with Excel or Minitab). There are new undergraduate and graduate surveys.

Chapter 2 This chapter has been completely reorganized. Section 1.5 of the previous edition, "Data Collection," has been moved to this chapter. This chapter opens by introducing the **DCOVA** approach (for **D**efine, **C**ollect, **O**rganize, **V**isualize, and **A**nalyze) for solving business problems. The material on tables and charts has been reorganized so that the sections on organizing data into tables is presented first, in Sections 2.2 and 2.3, followed by sections on visualizing data in graphs in Sections 2.4–2.7. There is a new section on organizing multidimensional data (Section 2.7) and new Excel and

Minitab Guide sections that discuss multidimensional data. There are also new examples throughout the chapter, and the chapter uses a new data set that contains a sample of 184 bond mutual funds.

Chapter 3 The section "Numerical Measures for a Population" has been moved after the section on quartiles and boxplots. For many examples, this chapter uses the new bond mutual funds data set that is introduced in Chapter 1.

Chapter 4 The chapter example has been updated. There are new problems throughout the chapter. The "Think About This" essay about Bayes' theorem has been condensed and updated. Counting rules have been added. In combinations and permutations, x is used instead of X to be consistent with binomial notation in Chapter 5.

Chapter 5 This chapter has revised notation for the binomial and Poisson distributions. It uses lower-case x and includes the parameter after an $|$ sign in the equation. To reduce the size of the book, the tables of the binomial and Poisson distributions (Tables E.6 and E.7) have been placed online. There are new problems throughout the chapter.

Chapter 6 This chapter has an updated Using Statistics scenario. The "Think About This" essay on the importance of the normal distribution has been revised.

Chapter 7 A new "Think About This" essay replaces and expands on the pros and cons of web-based surveys, using a famous historical example.

Chapter 8 This chapter includes problems on sigma known in Section 8.1.

Chapter 9 This chapter includes problems on sigma known in Section 9.1.

Chapter 10 This chapter has a new example on the paired t-test on textbook prices.

Chapter 11 This chapter has new problems throughout the chapter.

Chapter 12 The chapter now includes the section "Measuring Autocorrelation: The Durbin-Watson Statistic." The "Think About This" essay has been revised. There are new problems throughout the chapter.

Chapter 13 This chapter has various new problems.

Chapter 14 This chapter has been edited for conciseness without any loss of concepts or clarity. This chapter has been published as an online topic that is available for download from this book's download page. (To download this chapter, see the instructions in Appendix Section C.2 on page 534.)

Hallmark Features

We have continued many of the traditions of past editions and have highlighted some of these features below.

Using Statistics Business Scenarios—Each chapter begins with a Using Statistics example that shows how statistics is used in the functional areas of business—accounting, finance, information systems, management, and marketing. Each scenario is used throughout the chapter to provide an applied context for the concepts. The chapter concludes with a Using Statistics Revisited section that reinforces the statistical methods and applications discussed in each chapter.

Emphasis on Data Analysis and Interpretation of Software Results—We believe that the use of computer software is an integral part of learning statistics. Our focus emphasizes analyzing data by interpreting results while reducing emphasis on doing computations. For example, in the coverage of tables and charts in Chapter 2, the focus is on the interpretation of various charts and on when to use each chart. In our coverage of hypothesis testing in Chapters 9 through 11, and regression and multiple regression in Chapters 12 and 13, extensive computer results have been included so that the p-value approach can be emphasized.

Pedagogical Aids—An active writing style is used, with boxed numbered equations, set-off examples to provide reinforcement for learning concepts, problems divided into "Learning the Basics" and "Applying the Concepts," key equations, and key terms.

Answers—Many answers to the even-numbered exercises are included at the end of the book.

Flexibility Using Excel—For almost every statistical method discussed, this book presents more than one way of using Excel. Students can use *In-Depth Excel* instructions to directly work with worksheet solution details *or* they can use either the *PHStat2* instructions *or* the *Analysis ToolPak* instructions to automate the creation of those worksheet solutions.

Digital Cases—Digital Cases appear at the end of all chapters except Chapters 5 and 14. Most Digital Cases extend a Using Statistics business scenario by posing additional questions and raising issues about the scenario. Students examine interactive documents to sift through claims and assorted information in order to discover the data most relevant to a scenario. Students then determine whether the conclusions and claims are supported by the data. In doing so, students discover and learn how to identify common misuses of statistical information. (Instructional tips for using the Digital Cases and solutions to the Digital Cases are included in the Instructor's Solutions Manual.)

Case Studies and Team Projects—Detailed case studies are included in numerous chapters. A "Managing Ashland MultiComm Services" continuing case, a team project related to bond funds, and undergraduate and graduate student surveys are included at the end of most chapters, and these serve to integrate learning across the chapters.

Visual Explorations—The Excel add-in workbook allows students to interactively explore important statistical concepts in descriptive statistics, the normal distribution, sampling distributions, and regression analysis. For example, in descriptive statistics, students observe the effect of changes in the data on the mean, median, quartiles, and standard deviation. With the normal distribution, students see the effect of changes in the mean and standard deviation on the areas under the normal curve. In sampling distributions, students use simulation to explore the effect of sample size on a sampling distribution. In regression analysis, students have the opportunity to fit a line and observe how changes in the slope and intercept affect the goodness of fit.

Student Resources

Student Solutions Manual—Created by Professor Pin Tian Ng of Northern Arizona University, this manual provides detailed solutions to virtually all the even-numbered exercises and worked-out solutions to the self-test problems. Students can purchase this solutions manual by visiting **www.mypearsonstore.com** and searching for ISBN 0-13-280732-7. They can also purchase it at a reduced price when it is packaged with the text; search for ISBN 0-13-292479-X.

Online resources—This book comes with online resources that can be downloaded (see Appendix C that starts on page 534 for more details about these resources):

- **Data files** Excel and Minitab data files used by in-chapter examples and problems (in **.xls** and **.mtw** formats).
- **Online Chapter** The electronic-only Chapter 14: "Statistical Applications in Quality Management" in PDF format.
- **Excel Guide workbooks** Self-documenting Excel Guide workbooks illustrate solutions for more than 35 statistical topics that serve as freely reusable templates for future problem solving.
- **Case files** Supporting files are provided for the Digital Cases and the Managing Ashland MultiComm Services Case.
- **Visual Explorations** The files needed to use the Visual Explorations Excel add-in workbook.
- **Using Excel 2003 Guide** This guide presents, where necessary, alternate Excel Guide instructions for users of this older version of Excel.
- **PHStat2** The Pearson statistical add-in for Windows-based Excel 2003, 2007, and 2010. This version does not require the Excel Analysis ToolPak add-ins, thereby simplifying the installation and setup of this program.

MyStatLab™   *MyStatLab*—MyStatLab provides students with direct access to the online resources as well as the following exclusive online features and tools:

- **Interactive tutorial exercises** A comprehensive set of exercises have been written especially for use with this book that are algorithmically generated for unlimited practice and mastery.

Most exercises are free-response exercises and provide guided solutions, sample problems, and learning aids for extra help at point of use.

- **Personalized study plan** A plan indicates which topics have been mastered and creates direct links to tutorial exercises for topics that have not been mastered. MyStatLab manages the study plan, updating its content based on the results of online assessments.
- **Pearson Tutor Center (www.pearsontutorservices.com)** The MyStatlab student access code grants access to this online resource, staffed by qualified instructors who provide book-specific tutoring via phone, fax, e-mail, and interactive web sessions.
- **Integration with Pearson eTexts** iPad users can download a free app at **www.apple.com/ipad/apps-for-ipad/** and then sign in using their MyStatLab account to access a bookshelf of all their Pearson eTexts. The iPad app also allows access to the Do Homework, Take a Test, and Study Plan pages of their MyStatLab course.
- **Mobile Dashboard** Allows students to use their mobile devices to log in and review information from the dashboard of their courses: announcements, assignments, results, and progress bars for completed work. This app is available for iPhones, iPads, and Android phones, and is designed to promote effective study habits rather than to allow students to complete assignments on their mobile devices.

@RISK trial Palisade Corporation, the maker of the market-leading risk and decision analysis Excel add-ins, @RISK and the DecisionTools® Suite, provides special academic versions of its software to students (and faculty). Its flagship product, @RISK, debuted in 1987 and performs risk analysis using Monte Carlo simulation.

To download a trial version of @RISK software, visit **www.palisadecom/academic/**.

Instructor Resources

Instructor's Resource Center—Reached through a link at **www.pearsonhighered.com/levine**, the Instructor's Resource Center contains the electronic files for the complete Instructor's Solutions Manual, the Test Item File, and PowerPoint lecture presentations.

- **Register, redeem, log in** At **www.pearsonhighered.com/irc**, instructors can access a variety of print, media, and presentation resources that are available with this book in downloadable digital format. Resources are also available for course management platforms such as Blackboard, WebCT, and CourseCompass.
- **Need help?** Pearson Education's dedicated technical support team is ready to assist instructors with questions about the media supplements that accompany this text. Visit **http://247.pearsoned.com** for answers to frequently asked questions and toll-free user support phone numbers. The supplements are available to adopting instructors. Detailed descriptions are provided at the Instructor's Resource Center.

Instructor's Solutions Manual—Created by Professor Pin Tian Ng of Northern Arizona University and accuracy checked by Annie Puciloski, this manual includes solutions for end-of-section and end-of-chapter problems, answers to case questions, where applicable, and teaching tips for each chapter. The printed solutions are available by ordering ISBN 0-13-280729-7. Electronic solutions are provided at the Instructor's Resource Center in PDF and Word formats.

Lecture PowerPoint Presentations—PowerPoint presentations, created by Professor Patrick Schur of Miami University and accuracy checked by Annie Puciloski are available for each chapter at the Instructor's Resource Center. The PowerPoint slides provide an instructor with individual lecture outlines to accompany the text. The slides include many of the figures and tables from the text. Instructors can use these lecture notes as is or can easily modify the notes to reflect specific presentation needs.

Test Item File—Created by Professor Pin Tian Ng of Northern Arizona University and accuracy checked by Annie Puciloski, the Test Item File contains true/false, multiple-choice, fill-in, and problem-solving questions based on the definitions, concepts, and ideas developed in each chapter of the text. The Test Item File is available for download at the Instructor's Resource Center.

TestGen—Pearson Education's test-generating software is available from **www.pearsonhighered.com/irc**. The software is PC/Mac compatible and pre-loaded with all of the Test Item File questions. You can manually or randomly view test questions and drag and drop to create a test. You can add or modify test-bank questions as needed.

Learning Management Systems—Our TestGens are converted for use in BlackBoard and WebCT. These conversions can be found at the Instructor's Resource Center. Conversions to D2L or Angel can be requested through your local Pearson Sales Representative.

BlackBoard/WebCT—BlackBoard and WebCT Course Cartridges are available for download from **www.pearsonhighered.com/irc**. These standard course cartridges contain the Instructor's Solutions Manual, TestGen, PowerPoint Presentations, and Student Data Files.

MathXL®

MathXL for Statistics—MathXL for Statistics is a powerful online homework, tutorial, and assessment system that accompanies Pearson Education statistics textbooks. With MathXL for Statistics, instructors can create, edit, and assign online homework and tests using algorithmically generated exercises correlated at the objective level to the textbook. They can also create and assign their own online exercises and import TestGen tests for added flexibility. All student work is tracked in MathXL's online grade book. Students can take chapter tests in MathXL and receive personalized study plans based on their test results. Each study plan diagnoses weaknesses and links the student directly to tutorial exercises for the objectives he or she needs to study and retest. Students can also access supplemental animations and video clips directly from selected exercises. MathXL for Statistics is available to qualified adopters. For more information, visit **www.mathxl.com** or contact your sales representative.

MyStatLab™

MyStatLab—Part of the MyMathLab and MathXL product family, MyStatLab is a text-specific, easily customizable online course that integrates interactive multimedia instruction with textbook content. MyStatLab gives you the tools you need to deliver all or a portion of your course online, whether your students are in a lab setting or working from home. The latest version of MyStatLab offers a new, intuitive design that features more direct access to MathXL for Statistics pages (Gradebook, Homework & Test Manager, Home Page Manager, etc.) and provides enhanced functionality for communicating with students and customizing courses. Other key features include:

- **Assessment manager** An easy-to-use assessment manager lets instructors create online homework, quizzes, and tests that are automatically graded and correlated directly to your textbook. Assignments can be created using a mix of questions from the MyStatLab exercise bank, instructor-created custom exercises, and/or TestGen test items.
- **Grade book** Designed specifically for mathematics and statistics, the MyStatLab grade book automatically tracks students' results and gives you control over how to calculate final grades. You can also add offline (paper-and-pencil) grades to the grade book.
- **MathXL Exercise Builder** You can use the MathXL Exercise Builder to create static and algorithmic exercises for your online assignments. A library of sample exercises provides an easy starting point for creating questions, and you can also create questions from scratch.
- **eText-MathXL for Statistics Full Integration** Students using appropriate mobile devices can use your eText annotations and highlights for each course, and iPAd users can download a free app that allows them access to the Do Homework, Take a Test, and Study Plan pages of their course.
- **"Ask the Publisher" Link in "Ask My Instructor" Email** You can easily notify the content team of any irregularities with specific questions by using the "Ask the Publisher" functionality in the "Ask My Instructor" emails you receive from students.
- **Tracking Time Spent on Media** Because the latest version of MyStatLab requires students to explicitly click a "Submit" button after viewing the media for their assignments, you will be able to track how long students are spending on each media file.

Palisade Corporation software—Palisade Corporation, the maker of the market-leading risk and decision analysis Excel add-ins, @RISK and the DecisionTools® Suite, provides special academic versions of its software. Its flagship product, @RISK, debuted in 1987 and performs risk analysis using Monte Carlo simulation. With an estimated 150,000 users, Palisade software can be found in more than 100 countries and has been translated into five languages.

@RISK and the DecisionTools Suite are used widely in undergraduate and graduate business programs worldwide and can be bundled with this textbook. Thanks to the company's generous academic sales program, more than 40,000 students learn to make better decisions using @RISK and the DecisionTools Suite each year. To download a trial version of @RISK software, visit **www. palisade.com/academic/**.

Acknowledgments

We are extremely grateful to the RAND Corporation and the American Society for Testing and Materials for their kind permission to publish various tables in Appendix E, and the American Statistical Association for its permission to publish diagrams from the *American Statistician.*

A Note of Thanks

We would like to thank Levon R. Hayrapetyan, Houston Baptist University; Jim Mirabella, Jacksonville University; Adam Morris, Crowder College; Ravi Nath, Creighton University; Robert D. Patterson, Penn State-Erie–The Behrend College; Sulakshana Sen, Bethune Cookman University; and Kathryn A. Szabat, LaSalle University for their comments, which have made this a better book.

We would especially like to thank Chuck Synovec, Mary Kate Murray, Ashlee Bradbury, Judy Leale, Anne Fahlgren, and Jane Bonnell of the editorial, marketing, and production teams at Prentice Hall. We would like to thank our statistical reader and accuracy checker Annie Puciloski for her diligence in checking our work; Susan Pariseau, Merrimack College, for assisting in the reading of the page proofs; Julie Kennedy for her proofreading; and Lindsay Bethoney of PreMediaGlobal for her work in the production of this text.

Finally, we would like to thank our families for their patience, understanding, love, and assistance in making this book a reality. It is to them that we dedicate this book.

Concluding Remarks

We have gone to great lengths to make this text both pedagogically sound and error free. Please contact us at **davidlevine@davidlevinestatistics.com** if you require clarification about something discussed in this book, have a suggestion for a future edition, or if you discover an error. Include the phrase "BSFC edition 6" in the subject line of your e-mail. For technical support for PHStat2 beyond what is presented in the appendices and in the PHStat2 readme file that accompanies PHStat2, visit the PHStat2 website, **www.pearsonhighered.com/phstat** and click the **Contact Pearson Technical Support** link.

David M. Levine
Timothy C. Krehbiel
Mark L. Berenson

Business Statistics

A First Course

SIXTH EDITION

1 Introduction

Learning Objectives

In this chapter, you learn:

- What statistics is
- How statistics is fundamental to business
- The basic concepts and vocabulary of statistics
- How to use Microsoft Excel and/or Minitab with this book

maga/Shutterstock.com

@ GT&M Holdings

Managers at GT&M Holdings are worried about the financial health of their primary asset, the consumer electronics chain Good Tunes & More. The chain began as Good Tunes, a mail order retailer of music. In the early days of the Internet, managers made the strategic decision to move the business online, where Good Tunes prospered. Several years later, managers decided to open a physical "brick-and-mortar" store and the business changed into full-service consumer electronics retailer Good Tunes & More. During the last economic downturn, GT&M Holdings was able to take advantage of a depressed real estate market and store closings by some of their competitors to expand into a several-store chain.

Today, GT&M Holdings faces a number of challenges. In the short term, GT&M managers have to present relevant information to show their business is financially healthy and is worthy of new lines of credit. For the longer run, managers need to address the concerns of some private investors who have expressed concern about the long-term viability of Good Tunes & More. Managers will need to identify ways to enhance their business which, because it has evolved over many years, contains a patchwork of policies and practices that probably do not represent best practice and that may overlook opportunities for greater profits.

To face these challenges, GT&M managers will need to successfully apply the various business skills that their education and experience has given them. That much should be obvious. What may not be obvious is the role that statistics would play in applying those skills and making the decisions that will determine the future of Good Tunes & More.

Mihai Simonia/Photos.com

Statistics helps transform numbers into useful information for decision makers. Statistics lets you know about the risks associated with making a business decision and allows you to understand and reduce the variation in the decision-making process. **Descriptive statistics** are the methods that help collect, summarize, present, and analyze data. **Inferential statistics** are the methods that use the data collected from a small group to reach conclusions about a larger group. To use any method, you must first know if the method is appropriate for your data and whether any conditions or assumptions associated with a particular method have been met. In the GT&M Holdings scenario, managers will need to use both types of statistical methods to successfully face their challenges.

1.1 "Reading, Writing, and *Statistics?*"

No one undervalues how reading, writing, and basic math skills contribute to the academic success of a student (and people in business). And business students value the importance of having appropriate computer skills to support their studies and future jobs. But when the topic of statistics arises, some recall an introductory course that emphasized *descriptive* methods to summarize and present data, some express fear (after all, statistics *sounds* a lot like "sadistics"), and others will recall various sayings about statistics, the most famous of which may be "there are three types of lies: lies, damned lies, and statistics."[1]

Although often credited to Mark Twain, similar phrases appear in print at least a dozen years before Twain's phrase was recorded.

Many fail to realize that statistics is a core skill in their business education. As a core skill, statistics allows you to make better sense of the numbers used every day to describe and analyze the world. For example, in news stories such as these:

- **"More Clicks to Escape an Email List" (*The New York Times*, March 29, 2010, p. B2)** A study of 100 large online retailers reported that 39% required three or more clicks to opt out of an email list in 2009, compared to 7% in 2008.
- **"First Two years of College Wasted?" (M. Marklein, *USA Today*, January 18, 2011, p. 3A)** A survey of more than 3,000 full-time traditional-age students found that the students spent 51% of their time socializing, recreating, and other activities, 9% of their time attending class/lab, and 7% of their time studying.
- **"Follow the Tweets" (H. Rui, A. Whinston, and E. Winkler, *The Wall Street Journal*, November 30, 2009, p. R4)** In this study, the authors found that the number of times a specific product was mentioned in comments in the Twitter social messaging service could be used to make accurate predictions of sales trends for that product.

Statistics help you determine whether the "numbers" in these stories represent useful information. In doing that, statistics help you determine whether differences in the numbers are meaningful in a significant way or are just due to chance. Without statistics, you cannot see patterns in large amounts of data (e.g., that two-fifths of top retailers require three mouse click to unsubscribe from emails) and you cannot validate claims of causality such as that the number of Tweets can reflect sales of certain products.

For business students, statistics enhances their **numeracy**, or numerical literacy. Statistics plays such an important role in this way that, for business students, the "3Rs"—Reading, wRiting, and aRithmetic—might be better expressed as reading, writing, and statistics!

1.2 Statistics: Fundamental for Business

As a student, you probably had to take a "computer course," but probably did *not* expect to use computers *only* in that course. Likewise, from the points made in the previous section, you should start to realize that you will be using statistics in more than just your statistics course.

Statistics forms a fundamental part of the foundation of your business education because statistics plays a fundamental role in business. Statistics allows people in business to perform these important tasks:

- Visualize and summarize data (a use of descriptive methods)
- Reach conclusions about a large group based on data collected from a small group (a use of inferential methods)
- Make reliable forecasts from statistical models that infer information (another use of inferential methods)
- Improve business processes using managerial approaches such as Six Sigma that focus on quality improvement (a use of both descriptive and inferential methods)

How Statistics Has Become So Important

Statistics has become fundamental in business because of two long-term trends: the increasing accessibility of computerized statistical tools and increasing amounts of data that businesses can collect, store, and manage.

Once, developments in statistics were driven primarily by the needs of government to collect data on its citizenry. For example, in the United States, the U.S. Constitution requires a census be taken every 10 years. By the late nineteenth century, the growth of the U.S. population spurred the development of mechanical tabulating machines to record the census data and new descriptive statistics methods to present and summarize that data.

Starting also in the late nineteenth century were theoretical advances in mathematical probability theory that spurred the development of new inferential methods, especially methods of **statistical prediction** used to make reliable forecasts.[2] Initially, these methods were beyond the reach of the average person in business because of the complex calculations that these methods required. The early generations of business computers began to make these methods accessible to business at large but did not make them accessible to individual knowledge workers at their desktops in a timely fashion. Later, advances in personal computing and data communications, coupled with innovative software, made these methods immediately accessible on everyone's desktop.

More recently, advances in computing and data storage have permitted businesses to collect and process ever increasing amounts of data in ever decreasing amounts of time.[3] These advancements have spurred the development of new descriptive and inferential methods that form the emerging field of **analytics**. Analytics combines computer systems and statistics to generate new ways to help analyze corporate enterprise data, particularly collections of historical data. Analytics appears in many forms and as part of many types of modern managerial applications, including business intelligence, metrics, and current customer relationship management systems. Tom Davenport and Jeanne Harris, the authors of two recent books about this field, argue that using analytics should be part of the competitive strategy of an organization (see references 1 and 2). Whatever the actual future will bring, statistics will continue to be at least as important and fundamental as it is today.

Reconsidering the GT&M Holdings Scenario-I

As a small retail chain, Good Tunes & More uses computer systems for its daily operational activities such as recording sales and keeping track of inventory. Managers at GT&M Holdings can use descriptive statistical methods to tap into the data they collect as a result of these activities. With descriptive methods they could summarize and present the state of their business today—helpful to their short-term goal of securing credit. If Good Tunes & More were a larger firm, they might use a real-time analytic dashboard that would constantly update the status of their business. By using such a dashboard, managers would be better able to respond quickly to inventory, customer service, or other problems that might arise during a typical business day.

Do not confuse statistical prediction with the type of informal guessing that commentators use to "predict" the result of a sporting event or the winners of an entertainment industry awards show. Statistical prediction is a formal process used to infer information.

Changes in computing technology over time cannot be understated. Whereas a featured 1960s demonstration by the IBM Corporation retrieved and printed facts about a particular date submitted by audience members as they watched a 12-minute film (see reference 9), a 2011 demonstration had a computer system nicknamed "Watson" playing the quiz show Jeopardy! and deducing answers about a whole range of subjects in mere milliseconds (see reference 10).

1.3 Data and Variables

Already, several times in this chapter the word *data* has been used. The word is probably in your vocabulary and you already have the fuzzy sense that data is the "stuff" that statistics uses, but can you precisely define *data*? And is *data* a plural or singular in the English language? And does data always imply numbers being used? Just what is data?

Answering the last question is important because without a clear definition of the word some of the significant concepts in this book will remain fuzzy no matter how hard you study. For the purposes of this book, **data** are the *values* associated with a trait or property that help distinguish the occurrences of something. For example, "David Levine" and "Timothy Krehbiel" are values that help distinguish one of the authors of this book from another.

In this book, *data* is always plural to remind you that the data is a collection or set of values. While one could say that a single value such as "David Levine" is a *datum*, the phrases *data point*, *observation*, *response*, or *single data value* are more typically used to describe a single value. (If you have used *data* as a singular, you were probably thinking about the entire collection or set of values, which, after all, is a single thing. In this book, "a set of data," "data file," or "file" are the phrases used to refer to the entire collection.)

Being clear about the meaning of *data* helps to define the term **variable**. A variable is one of those traits or properties that helps distinguish the occurrence of something. In the previous example, "David Levine" and "Timothy Krehbiel" are values for a variable that could be called Name or Author Name. Substituting the word *characteristic* for the phrase "trait or property that helps distinguish" and substituting the phrase "an item or individual" for the word *something* produces the standard statistical definitions of *variable* and *data*.

> ### VARIABLE
> A characteristic of an item or individual.
>
> ### DATA
> The set of individual values associated with a variable.

Each variable you use must have an **operational definition**. An operational definition allows all associated with an analysis to understand what the variable represents and what its possible values are. For example, in a famous example, researchers collecting demographic data asked persons to fill in a form, one line of which asked about Sex. More than one person filled in the answer Yes and not the Male or Female that the researchers sought. (Perhaps this is the reason that this variable is typically named Gender—gender's operational definition is more self-apparent.)

Operational definitions sometimes need to define individual values as well. For example, for a class standing variable defined to take one of the four values freshman, sophomore, junior, and senior, each of those *values* would need to be defined (perhaps in terms of credits earned) in order to ensure that everyone had a common understanding. Perhaps the most famous example of vague definitions for values was the 2000 U.S. presidential election in the state of Florida in which the definitions for "valid" and "invalid" ballots were the subject of controversy.

Types of Variables

The nature of the data associated with a variable determines type. Knowing the variable type is important because the statistical methods you can use in your analysis vary according to type.

Categorical variables (also known as **qualitative variables**) have values that can only be placed into categories such as yes and no. "Do you currently own bonds?" (yes or no) and the level of risk of a bond fund (below average, average, or above average) are examples of categorical variables.

Numerical variables (also known as **quantitative variables**) have values that represent quantities. Numerical variables are further identified as being either *discrete* or *continuous* variables.

Discrete variables have numerical values that arise from a counting process. "The number of premium cable channels subscribed to" is an example of a discrete numerical variable because the response is one of a finite number of integers. You subscribe to zero, one, two, or more channels. "The number of items purchased" is also a discrete numerical variable because you are counting the number of items purchased.

Continuous variables produce numerical responses that arise from a measuring process. The time you wait for teller service at a bank is an example of a continuous numerical variable because the response takes on any value within a *continuum*, or an interval, depending on the precision of the measuring instrument. For example, your waiting time could be 1 minute, 1.1 minutes, 1.11 minutes, or 1.113 minutes, depending on the precision of the measuring device used. (Theoretically, no two continuous values would ever be identical. However, because no measuring device is perfectly precise, identical continuous values for two or more items or individuals can occur.)

At first glance, identifying the variable type may seem easy, but some variables that you might want to study could be either categorical or numerical, depending on how you define them. For example, "age" would seem to be an obvious numerical variable, but what if you are interested in comparing the buying habits of children, young adults, middle-aged persons, and retirement-age people? In that case, defining "age" as a categorical variable would make better sense. Again, this illustrates the earlier point that without operational definitions, variables are meaningless.

Asking questions about the variables you have identified for study can often be a great help in determining the variable type you want. Table 1.1 illustrates the process.

TABLE 1.1

Types of Variables

Question	Responses	Data Type
Do you currently have a profile on Facebook?	❑ Yes ❑ No ⟶	Categorical
How many text messages have you sent in the past week?	____ ⟶	Numerical (discrete)
How long did it take to download a video game?	____ seconds ⟶	Numerical (continuous)

1.4 Basic Vocabulary of Statistics

Learning about the statistical methods discussed in this book is nearly impossible if you do not first understand the meaning of four terms: *population, sample, parameter,* and *statistic* (singular).

Data arises from either a *population* or a *sample*. A **population** consists all the items or individuals about which you want to reach conclusions. All of the Good Tunes & More sales transactions for a specific year, all the customers who shopped at Good Tunes & More this weekend, all the full-time students enrolled in a college, and all the registered voters in Ohio are examples of populations.

A **sample** is a portion of a population selected for analysis. From the four examples of populations just given, you could select a sample of 200 Good Tunes & More sales transactions randomly selected by an auditor for study, a sample of 30 Good Tunes & More customers asked to complete a customer satisfaction survey, a sample of 50 full-time students selected for a marketing study, and a sample of 500 registered voters in Ohio contacted via telephone for a political poll. In each of these examples, the transactions or people in the sample represent a portion of the items or individuals that make up the population.

The other two basic terms, *parameter* and *statistic*, are measures that help describe the data associated with a variable. A **parameter** is a measure that describes a variable that uses population data. A statistic is a measure that describes a variable that uses sample data. The average amount of a Good Tunes & More sales transactions for a specific year is an example of a parameter because the measure, average amount, describes data from a population, all of the transactions for a specific year. In contrast, the average amount of the 200 Good Tunes & More sales transactions randomly selected by an auditor for study is an example of a statistic because the measure describes data from a sample.

As done in the summary definitions that follow, parameter and statistic can also be defined using the word characteristic and avoiding explicit references to variables.

BASIC VOCABULARY OF STATISTICS

A **population** consists of all the items or individuals about which you want to reach conclusions.

A **sample** is the portion of a population selected for analysis.

A **parameter** is a measure that describes a characteristic of a population.

A **statistic** is a measure that describes a characteristic of a sample.

Problems for Section 1.4

LEARNING THE BASICS

1.1 Four different beverages are sold at a fast-food restaurant: soft drinks, tea, coffee, and bottled water.

Explain why the type of beverage sold is an example of a categorical variable.

1.2 Soft drinks are sold in three sizes at a fast-food restaurant: small, medium, and large. Explain why the size of a soft drink is an example of a categorical variable.

1.3 Suppose that you measure the time it takes to download a video from the Internet.

Explain why the download time is a continuous numerical variable.

APPLYING THE CONCEPTS

✓SELF Test **1.4** For each of the following variables, determine whether the variable is categorical or numerical. If the variable is numerical, determine whether the variable is discrete or continuous.

a. Number of landline telephones in the household

b. Length (in minutes) of the longest telephone call made in a month

c. Whether someone in the household owns a Wi-Fi-capable cell phone

d. Whether there is a high-speed Internet connection in the household

e. Whether telephone service in the household is provided by the household's Internet provider

f. Number of cellphones in the household

1.5 The following information is collected from students upon exiting the campus bookstore during the first week of classes.

a. Amount of time spent shopping in the bookstore

b. Number of textbooks purchased

c. Academic major

d. Gender

Classify each of these variables as categorical or numerical. If the variable is numerical, determine whether the variable is discrete or continuous.

1.6 For each of the following variables, determine whether the variable is categorical or numerical. If the variable is numerical, determine whether the variable is discrete or continuous.

a. Name of Internet service provider
b. Time in hours spent surfing the Internet per week
c. Number of text messages sent in a week
d. Number of online purchases made in a month
e. Whether the individual has a Facebook profile

1.7 For each of the following variables, determine whether the variable is categorical or numerical. If the variable is numerical, determine whether the variable is discrete or continuous.
a. Amount of money spent on clothing in the past month
b. Favorite department store
c. Most likely time period during which shopping for clothing takes place (weekday, weeknight, or weekend)
d. Number of pairs of shoes owned

1.8 Suppose the following information is collected from Robert Keeler on his application for a home mortgage loan at the Metro County Savings and Loan Association.
a. Monthly payments: $1,927
b. Number of jobs in past 10 years: 1
c. Annual family income: $76,000
d. Marital status: Married
Classify each of the responses by type of data

1.9 One of the variables most often included in surveys is income. Sometimes the question is phrased "What is your income (in thousands of dollars)?" In other surveys, the respondent is asked to "Select the circle corresponding to your income level" and is given a number of income ranges to choose from.
a. In the first format, explain why income might be considered either discrete or continuous.
b. Which of these two formats would you prefer to use if you were conducting a survey? Why?

1.10 If two students score a 90 on the same examination, what arguments could be used to show that the underlying variable—test score—is continuous?

1.11 The director of market research at a large department store chain wanted to conduct a survey throughout a metropolitan area to determine the amount of time working women spend shopping for clothing in a typical month.
a. Describe both the population and the sample of interest. Indicate the type of data the director might want to collect.
b. Develop a first draft of the questionnaire needed in (a) by writing three categorical questions and three numerical questions that you feel would be appropriate for this survey.

1.5 Statistical Applications for Desktop Computing

Advances in computing during the past 40 years have brought statistical computing to the business desktop. Statistical functionality is so commonplace today that many simple statistical tasks once done exclusively with pencil and paper or hand calculators are now done electronically, with the assistance of statistical applications.

Excel and Minitab are examples of desktop applications that people use for statistics. Excel is the Microsoft Office data analysis application that evolved from earlier electronic spreadsheets used in accounting and financial applications. Minitab, a dedicated statistical application, or **statistical package**, was developed from the ground up to perform statistical analysis as accurately as possible. Versions of Minitab run on larger computer systems and can perform heavy-duty corporate analyses involving very large data sets. Excel and Minitab are two very different programs, and their differences have led to an ongoing debate as to which program is more appropriate for use in an introductory business statistics course. Proponents of each program point to their program's strengths: Minitab as a complete statistical solution; Excel as a common desktop tool found in many businesses (and in many different business schools).

Although you are probably more familiar with Excel than with Minitab, both programs share many similarities, starting with their shared use of **worksheets** (or spreadsheets) to store data for analysis. Worksheets are tabular arrangements of data, in which the intersections of rows and columns form **cells**, boxes into which you make entries. In Minitab, the data for each variable are placed in separate columns, and this is also the standard practice when using Excel. Generally, to perform a statistical analysis in either program, you select one or more columns of data and then apply the appropriate command.

Both Excel and Minitab allow you to save worksheets, programming information, and results as one file, called a **workbook** in Excel and a **project** in Minitab. In Excel, workbooks are collections of worksheets and chart sheets. You save a workbook when you save "an Excel file" (as either an **.xls** or **.xlsx** file). In Minitab, a project includes data worksheets, all the results shown in a **session window**, and all graphs created for the data. Unlike in Excel, in Minitab you can save individual worksheets (as **.mtw** worksheet files) as well as save the entire project (as an **.mpj** project file).

You can use either Excel or Minitab to learn and practice the statistical methods learned in this book. The end of each chapter presents guides that contain detailed instructions for applying Microsoft Excel and Minitab to the statistical methods taught in the chapter. These Excel and Minitab Guides use some of the downloadable files discussed in Appendix C to illustrate the step-by-step process by which you apply a method. The Excel Guides additionally offer a choice of techniques—all leading to the same results—that allow you to use Excel either in a semi-automated way to get quick results or as a "sandbox" in which you construct results from scratch or from model templates. This is further explained in Section EG1.1 of the Chapter 1 Excel Guide.

1.6 How to Use This Book

This book organizes its material around the four important uses of statistics in business (see Section 1.2). Chapters 2 and 3 present methods that summarize business data to address the first task listed. Chapters 4 through 11 discuss methods that use sample data to draw conclusions about populations (the second task). Chapters 12 and 13 review methods to make reliable forecasts (the third task). Chapter 14 introduces methods that you can use to improve business processes (the fourth task). In addition, Chapter 2 introduces a problem-solving approach that will help you learn individual methods and help you apply your knowledge beyond the statistics course.

To help you develop and integrate these skills, which will give you a basis for making better decisions, each chapter of *Business Statistics: A First Course* begins with a Using Statistics scenario. Each scenario describes a realistic business situation and raises questions that help introduce the use of specific statistical concepts or methods. For example, the GT&M Holdings in this chapter introduces the types of statistical methods and some of the issues involving variable definition. In other chapters, scenarios raise more specific concerns in the form of questions such as "Which location in a supermarket best enhances sales of a cola drink?" or "Does the size of a retail store influence sales?"

The end of each chapter revisits the chapter's scenario to describe how specific methods discussed in the chapter could be used to help answer the questions raised in the scenario. Also included at the end of each chapter are sections such as Summary, Key Terms, Key Equations, and Chapter Review Problems that help you review what you have learned.

Following this review material in most chapters, you will find a continuing case study that allows you to apply statistics to problems faced by the management of Ashland MultiComm Services, a residential telecommunications provider. Most chapters also contain a Digital Case, in which you examine a variety of electronic documents and apply your statistical knowledge to resolve problems or address issues raised by these cases. Many of the Digital Cases will help you think about what constitutes the proper or ethical use of statistics. ("Learning with the Digital Cases" on page 14 introduces you to this unique set of business cases.) Finally, at the very end of each chapter, except for the last chapter, are the Excel Guides and Minitab Guides discussed in Section 1.5.

Don't worry if your instructor does not cover every section of every chapter. Introductory business statistics courses vary in their scope, length, and number of college credits. Your chosen functional area of specialization (accounting, management, finance, marketing, etc.) may also affect what you learn in class or what you are assigned or choose to read in this book.

Checklist for Getting Started

To make the best use of this book, you need to work with Excel or Minitab and download and use files and other electronic resources that are available from this book's download page (discussed fully in Appendix C). To minimize problems you may face later when using these resources, review and complete the Table 1.2 checklist. When you have checked off all the tasks necessary for your own work, you will be ready to begin reading the Chapter 1 Excel or Minitab Guide and using the supplemental material in Appendices B, C, D, F and G, as necessary.

TABLE 1.2

Checklist for Getting Started with *Business Statistics: A First Course*

❑ Select which program, Excel or Minitab, you will use with this book. (Your instructor may have made this decision for you.)

❑ Read Appendix A if you need to learn or review basic math concepts and notation.

❑ Read Appendix B if you need to learn or review basic computing concepts and skills.

❑ Download the files and other electronic resources needed to work with this book. Read Appendix C to learn more about the things you can download from the download page for this book. (This process requires Internet access.)

❑ Successfully install the chosen program and apply all available updates to the program. Read Appendix Section D.1 to learn how to find and apply updates. (This process requires Internet access.)

❑ If you plan to use PHStat2 with Excel, complete the special checklist in Appendix Section D.2. If you plan to use the Analysis ToolPak with Excel, read and follow the instructions in Appendix Section D.5.

❑ Skim Appendices F and G to be aware of how these appendices can help you as you use this book with Excel or Minitab.

When you have completed the checklist, you are ready to begin using the Excel Guides and Minitab Guides that appear at the end of chapters. These guides discuss how to apply Excel and Minitab to the statistical methods discussed in the chapter. The Excel Guides and Minitab Guides for this chapter (which begin on pages 16 and 21, respectively) review the basic operations of these programs and explain how Excel and Minitab handle the concept of type of variable discussed in Section 1.3.

Instructions in the Excel Guides and Minitab Guides and related appendices use the conventions for computer operations presented in Table 1.3. Read and review Appendix B if some of the vocabulary used in the table is new to you.

TABLE 1.3

Conventions for Computing Operations

Operation	Examples	Interpretation
Keyboard keys	**Enter** **Ctrl** **Shift**	Names of keys are always the object of the verb *press*, as in "press **Enter**."
Keystroke combination	**Crtl+C** **Crtl+Shift+Enter**	Some keyboarding actions require you to press more than one key at the same time. **Crtl+C** means press the **C** key while holding down the **Ctrl** key. **Crtl+Shift+Enter** means press the **Enter** key while holding down the **Ctrl** and **Shift** keys.
Click object	Click **OK**. Click **All** in the **Page Range** section.	A *click object* is a target of a mouse click. When click objects are part of a window that contains more than one part, the part name is also given, e.g., "in the **Page Range** section." Review Appendix Section B.2 to learn the verbs this book uses with click objects.
Menu or ribbon selection	**File → New** **Layout →** **Trendline →** **Linear Trendline**	A sequence of menu or ribbon selections is represented by a list of choices separated by the → symbol. **File → New** means first select **File** and then, from the list of choices that appears, select **New**.
Placeholder object	Select *variablename*	An italicized object means that the actual object varies, depending on the context of the instruction. "Select *variablename*" might, for one problem, mean "select the **Yearly Sales** variable" and might mean "select the **Monthly Sales** variable" for another.

USING STATISTICS @ GT&M Holdings Revisited

maga/Shutterstock.com

I n the GT&M Holdings scenario, managers faced both short-term and longer-term issues. To help address those issues, managers need to employ statistical methods in a proper way. Their first task is to identify and define variables that are relevant to those issues. Because some of the variables they would identify have thousands of data values, the managers need to learn ways to organize, summarize, and present those variables (the subject matter of Chapter 2).

SUMMARY

Statistics is the collection of methods that help you make better sense of the data used every day to describe and analyze the world. Statistics is a core skill necessary for a complete business education. Businesses use statistics to summarize and reach conclusions from data, to make reliable forecasts, and to improve business processes. In this

chapter, you learned the basic vocabulary of statistics and the various types of data used in business. In the next two chapters, you will study data collection and a variety of tables and charts and descriptive measures that are used to present and analyze data.

KEY TERMS

analytics   5
categorical variable   6
continuous variable   7
data   6
descriptive statistics   4
discrete variable   7
inferential statistics   4

numeracy   4
numerical variable   7
operational definition   6
parameter   8
population   7
qualitative variable   6
quantitative variable   7

sample   8
statistic   8
statistical package   9
statistical prediction   5
statistics   4
variable   6

CHAPTER REVIEW PROBLEMS

CHECKING YOUR UNDERSTANDING

1.12 What is the difference between a sample and a population?

1.13 What is the difference between a statistic and a parameter?

1.14 What is the difference between descriptive statistics and inferential statistics?

1.15 What is the difference between a categorical variable and a numerical variable?

1.16 What is the difference between a discrete numerical variable and a continuous numerical variable?

1.17 What is an operational definition, and why are operational definitions so important?

1.18 What is the difference between a variable and data?

APPLYING THE CONCEPTS

1.19 Visit the official website for either Excel or Minitab, **www.office.microsoft.com/excel** or **www.minitab.com/products/minitab**. Read about the program you chose and then think about the ways the program could be useful in statistical analysis.

1.20 In 2008, a university in the midwestern United States surveyed its full-time first-year students after they completed their first semester. Surveys were electronically distributed to all 3,727 students, and responses were obtained from 2,821 students. Of the students surveyed, 90.1% indicated that they had studied with other students, and 57.1% indicated that they had tutored another student. The report also noted that 61.3% of the students surveyed came to class late at least once, and 45.8% admitted to being bored in class at least once.
a. Describe the population of interest.
b. Describe the sample that was collected.

c. Describe a parameter of interest.

d. Describe the statistic used to estimate the parameter in (c).

1.21 The Gallup organization releases the results of recent polls at its website, **www.gallup.com**. Visit this site and read an article of interest.

a. Describe the population of interest.

b. Describe the sample that was collected.

c. Describe a parameter of interest.

d. Describe the statistic used to describe the parameter in (c).

1.22 A Gallup poll indicated that 74% of Americans who had yet to retire look to retirement accounts as major funding sources when they retire. Interestingly, 40% also said that they looked to stocks or stock market mutual fund investments as major funding sources when they retire. (data extracted from D. Jacobs, "Investors Look Beyond Social Security to Fund Retirement," **www.gallup.com**, March 28, 2011). The results are based on telephone interviews conducted March 24, 2011, with 1,000 or more adults living in the United States, aged 18 and older.

a. Describe the population of interest.

b. Describe the sample that was collected.

c. Is 74% a parameter or a statistic? Explain.

d. Is 40% a parameter or a statistic?

1.23 The Data and Story Library (DASL) is an online library of data files and stories that illustrate the use of basic statistical methods. Visit **lib.stat.cmu.edu/index.php**, click DASL and explore a data set of interest to you.

a. Describe a variable in the data set you selected.

b. Is the variable categorical or numerical?

c. If the variable is numerical, is it discrete or continuous?

1.24 Download and examine the U.S. Census Bureau's "2007 Survey of Business Owners and Self-Employed Persons," directly available at **bhs.econ.census.gov/BHS/SBO/sbo1_07.pdf** or through the **Get Help with Your Form** link at **www.census.gov/econ/sbo**.

a. Give an example of a categorical variable included in the survey.

b. Give an example of a numerical variable included in the survey.

1.25 Three professors at Northern Kentucky University compared two different approaches to teaching courses in the school of business (M. W. Ford, D. W. Kent, and S. Devoto, "Learning from the Pros: Influence of Web-Based Expert Commentary on Vicarious Learning About Financial Markets," *Decision Sciences Journal of Innovative Education*, January 2007, 5(1), 43–63). At the time of the study, there were 2,100 students in the business school, and 96 students were involved in the study. Demographic data collected on these 96 students included class (freshman, sophomore, junior, senior), age, gender, and major.

a. Describe the population of interest.

b. Describe the sample that was collected.

c. Indicate whether each of the four demographic variables mentioned is categorical or numerical.

1.26 A manufacturer of cat food was planning to survey households in the United States to determine purchasing habits of cat owners. Among the variables to be collected are the following:

   i. The primary place of purchase for cat food

   ii. Whether dry or moist cat food is purchased

   iii. The number of cats living in the household

   iv. Whether any cat living in the household is pedigreed

a. For each of the four items listed, indicate whether the variable is categorical or numerical. If it is numerical, is it discrete or continuous?

b. Develop five categorical questions for the survey.

c. Develop five numerical questions for the survey.

1.27 A sample of 62 undergraduate students answered the following survey:

 1. What is your gender? Female _____ Male _____

 2. What is your age (*as of last birthday*)? _____

 3. What is your current registered class designation? Freshman _____ Sophomore _____ Junior _____ Senior _____

 4. What is your major area of study? Accounting _____ Computer Information Systems _____ Economics/Finance _____ International Business _____ Management _____ Retailing/Marketing _____ Other _____ Undecided _____

 5. At the present time, do you plan to attend graduate school? Yes _____ No _____ Not sure _____

 6. What is your current cumulative grade point average? _____

 7. What is your current employment status? Full time _____ Part time _____ Unemployed _____

 8. What would you expect your starting annual salary (*in $000*) to be if you were to seek full-time employment immediately after obtaining your bachelor's degree? _____

 9. For how many social networking sites are you registered? _____

10. How satisfied are you with the food and dining services on campus? _____

	1	2	3	4	5	6	7	
Extremely unsatisfied			Neutral				Extremely satisfied	

11. About how much money did you spend this semester for textbooks and supplies? _____

12. What type of computer do you prefer to use for your studies? Desktop _____ Laptop _____ Tablet/notebook/netbook _____

13. How many text messages do you send in a typical week? _____

14. How much wealth (income, savings, investment, real estate, and other assets) would you have to accumulate (in millions of dollars) before you would say you are rich? _____

a. Which variables in the survey are categorical?

b. Which variables in the survey are numerical?

c. Which variables are discrete numerical variables?

The results of the survey are stored in `UndergradSurvey`

1.28 A sample of 44 graduate students answered the following survey:

1. What is your gender? Female _____ Male _____
2. What is your age (*as of last birthday*)? _____
3. What is your current major area of study?
   Accounting _____
   Economics/Finance _____
   Management _____
   Retailing/Marketing _____
   Other _____ Undecided _____
4. What is your current graduate cumulative grade point average? _____
5. What was your undergraduate major?
   Biological Sciences _____ Business _____
   Computers _____
   Engineering _____
   Other _____
6. What was your undergraduate cumulative grade point average? _____
7. What is your current employment status?
   Full time _____ Part time _____ Unemployed _____

8. How many different full-time jobs have you held in the past 10 years? _____
9. What do you expect your annual salary (*in $000*) to be immediately after completion of your graduate studies if you are employed full time? _____
10. About how much money did you spend this semester for textbooks and supplies? _____
11. How satisfied are you with the MBA program advisory services on campus?

            1   2   3   4   5   6   7

    Extremely   Neutral   Extremely
    unsatisfied   satisfied
12. What type of computer do you prefer to use for your studies?
    Desktop _____ Laptop _____ Tablet/notebook/ netbook _____
13. How many text messages do you send in a typical week? _____
14. How much wealth (income, savings, investment, real estate, and other assets) would you have to accumulate (in millions of dollars) before you would say you are rich? _____

    a. Which variables in the survey are categorical?

    b. Which variables in the survey are numerical?

    c. Which variables are discrete numerical variables?

The results of the survey are stored in `GradSurvey`

END-OF-CHAPTER CASES

At the end of most chapters, you will find a continuing case study that allows you to apply statistics to problems faced by the management of the Ashland MultiComm Services, a residential telecommunications provider. You will also find a series of Digital Cases that extend many of the Using Statistics scenarios that begin each chapter.

LEARNING WITH THE DIGITAL CASES

People use statistical techniques to help communicate and present important information to others both inside and outside their businesses. Every day, as in these examples, people misuse these techniques. Identifying and preventing misuses of statistics, whether intentional or not, is an important responsibility for all managers. The Digital Cases help you develop the skills necessary for this important task.

A Digital Case asks you to review electronic documents related to a company or statistical issue discussed in the chapter's Using Statistics scenario. You review the contents of these documents, which may contain internal confidential as well as publicly stated facts and claims, seeking to identify and correct misuses of statistics. Unlike a traditional case study, but like many business situations, not all of the information you encounter will be relevant to your task, and you may occasionally discover conflicting

information that you have to resolve in order to complete the case.

To assist your learning, each Digital Case begins with a learning objective and a summary of the problem or issue at hand. Each case directs you to the information necessary to reach your own conclusions and to answer the case questions. You can work with the documents for the Digital Cases offline, after downloading them from this book's download page (see Appendix C). Or you can work with the Digital Cases online, chapter-by-chapter, at the companion website.

DIGITAL CASE EXAMPLE

This section illustrates learning with a Digital Case. To begin, open the Digital Case file **GTM.pdf**, which contains contents from the Good Tunes & More website. Recall that the privately held Good Tunes & More, the subject of the

Using Statistics scenario in this chapter, is seeking financing to expand its business by opening retail locations. Because the managers are eager to show that Good Tunes & More is a thriving business, it is not surprising to discover the "our best sales year ever" claim in the "Good Times at Good Tunes & More" section on the first page.

Click the **our best sales year ever** link to display the page that supports this claim. How would you support such a claim? With a table of numbers? A chart? Remarks attributed to a knowledgeable source? Good Tunes & More has used a chart to present "two years ago" and "latest twelve months" sales data by category. Are there any problems with the choices made on this web page? *Absolutely!*

First, note that there are no scales for the symbols used, so it is impossible to know what the actual sales volumes are. In fact, as you will learn in Section 2.8, charts that incorporate symbols in this way are considered examples of *chartjunk* and would never be used by people seeking to properly use graphs.

This important point aside, another question that arises is whether the sales data represent the number of units sold or something else. The use of the symbols creates the impression that unit sales data are being presented. If the data are unit sales, does such data best support the claim being made, or would something else, such as dollar volumes, be a better indicator of sales at the retailer?

Then there are those curious chart labels. "Latest twelve months" is ambiguous; it could include months from the current year as well as months from one year ago and therefore may not be an equivalent time period to "two years ago." But the business was established in 1997, and the claim being made is "best sales year ever," so why hasn't management included sales figures for *every* year?

Are Good Tunes & More managers hiding something, or are they just unaware of the proper use of statistics? Either way, they have failed to properly communicate a vital aspect of their story.

In subsequent Digital Cases, you will be asked to provide this type of analysis, using the open-ended questions in the case as your guide. Not all the cases are as straightforward as this example, and some cases include perfectly appropriate applications of statistics.

REFERENCES

1. Davenport, T., and J. Harris, *Competing on Analytics: The New Science of Winning* (Boston: Harvard Business School Press, 2007).
2. Davenport, T., J. Harris, and R. Morrison, *Analytics at Work* (Boston: Harvard Business School Press, 2010).
3. McCullough, B. D., and D. Heiser, "On the Accuracy of Statistical Procedures in Microsoft Excel 2007," *Computational Statistics and Data Analysis*, 52 (2008), 4568–4606.
4. McCullough, B. D., and B. Wilson, "On the Accuracy of Statistical Procedures in Microsoft Excel 97," *Computational Statistics and Data Analysis*, 31 (1999), 27–37.
5. McCullough, B. D., and B. Wilson, "On the Accuracy of Statistical Procedures in Microsoft Excel 2003," *Computational Statistics and Data Analysis*, 49 (2005), 1244–1252.
6. *Microsoft Excel 2010* (Redmond, WA: Microsoft Corporation, 2010).
7. *Minitab Release 16* (State College, PA: Minitab, Inc., 2010).
8. Nash, J. C., "Spreadsheets in Statistical Practice—Another Look," *The American Statistician*, 60 (2006), 287–289.
9. New York 1964 World's Fair," *National Geographic*, April 1965, p. 526
10. Thompson, C. "What Is I.B.M.'s Watson?". **http://www.nytimes.com/2010/06/20/magazine/20Computer-t.html**, June 20, 2010, p. MM30 of the Sunday Magazine.

CHAPTER 1 EXCEL GUIDE

EG1.1 GETTING STARTED with EXCEL

You are almost ready to use Excel if you have completed the Table 1.2 checklist and reviewed the Table 1.3 conventions for computing on page 11. Before going further, decide how you plan to use Excel with this book. The Excel Guides include *In-Depth Excel* instructions that require no additional software and *PHStat2* instructions that use PHStat2, an add-in that simplifies using Excel while creating results identical to those you would get using the Excel instructions. Table EG1.1 lists the advantages and disadvantages of each type of instruction. Because of the equivalency of these two types, you can switch between them at any time while using this book.

TABLE EG1.1

Types of Excel Guide Instructions

In-Depth Excel Instructions
Provides step-by-step instructions for applying Excel to the statistical methods of the chapter.   **Advantages** Applicable to all Excel versions. Creates "live" worksheets and chart sheets that automatically update when the underlying data change.   **Disadvantages** Can be time-consuming, frustrating, and error prone, especially for novices. May force you to focus on low-level Excel details, thereby distracting you from learning statistics.

PHStat2 Instructions
Provides step-by-step instructions for using the PHStat2 add-in with Excel. (To learn more about PHStat2, see Appendix G.)   **Advantages** Creates live worksheets and chart sheets that are the same as or similar to the ones created in the *In-Depth Excel* instructions. Frees you from having to focus on low-level Excel details. Can be used to quickly double-check results created by the *In-Depth Excel* instructions.   **Disadvantages** Must be installed separately and therefore requires an awareness about installing software on your system. (See Appendix D for the technical details.) Not compatible with Mac OS versions of Excel.

If you want to develop a mastery of Excel and gain practice building solutions from the bottom up, you will want to use the *In-Depth Excel* instructions. If you are more of a top-down person, who first wants quick results and then, later, looks at the details of a solution, you will want to maximize your use of the *PHStat2* instructions. At any time, you can switch between these methods without any loss of comprehension. Both methods lead to identical, or nearly identical, results. These results are mostly in the form of reusable workbooks. These workbooks, as well as the workbooks you can download (see Appendix C) are yours to keep and reuse for other problems, in other courses, or in your workplace.

When relevant, the Excel Guides also include instructions for the Analysis ToolPak, an optional component of Excel that Microsoft distributes with many versions of Excel, although not with the current version of Mac Excel.

The Excel Guide instructions feature Windows Excel versions 2010 and 2007 and note their differences, when those differences are significant. The instructions have been written for maximum compatibility with current versions of Mac Excel and OpenOffice.org Calc, an Excel work-alike. If you use either Mac Excel or OpenOffice.org Calc, you will be able to use almost all the workbooks discussed in the *In-Depth Excel* instructions. If you use the older Windows-based Excel 2003, you can use the *PHStat2* instructions as is and can download from this book's companion website the *Using Excel 2003 with Basic Business Statistics* document that adapts the *In-Depth Excel* instructions for use with Excel 2003.

The rest of this Excel Guide reviews the basic concepts and common operations encountered when using Excel with this book.

EG1.2 ENTERING DATA and VARIABLE TYPE

As first discussed in Section 1.5, you enter the data for each variable in a separate column. By convention, you start with column A and enter the name of each variable into the cells of the first row, and then you enter the data for the variable in the subsequent rows, as shown in Figure EG1.1.

FIGURE EG1.1

An example of a data worksheet

	A	B	C	D	E	F	G	H	I
1	Fund Number	Type	Assets	Fees	Expense Ratio	Return 2009	3-Year Return	5-Year Return	Risk
2	FN-1	Intermediate Government	7268.1	No	0.45	6.9	6.9	5.5	Below average
3	FN-2	Intermediate Government	475.1	No	0.50	9.8	7.5	6.1	Below average
4	FN-3	Intermediate Government	193.0	No	0.71	6.3	7.0	5.6	Average
5	FN-4	Intermediate Government	18602.5	No	0.13	5.4	6.6	5.5	Average

Excel infers the variable type from the data you enter into a column. If Excel discovers a column containing numbers, for example, it treats the column as a numerical variable. If Excel discovers a column containing words or alphanumeric entries, it treats the column as a non-numerical (categorical) variable. This imperfect method works most of the time in Excel, especially if you make sure that the categories for your categorical variables are words or phrases such as "yes" and "no" and are not coded values that could be mistaken for numerical values, such as "1," "2," and "3." However, because you cannot explicitly define the variable type, Excel occasionally makes "mistakes" by either offering or allowing you to do nonsensical things such as using a statistical method that is designed for numerical variables on categorical variables.

When you enter data, never skip any rows in a column, and as a general rule, also avoid skipping any columns. Pay attention to any special instructions that occur throughout the book for the order of the entry of your data. For some statistical methods, entering your data in an order that Excel does not expect will lead to incorrect results.

Most of the Excel workbooks that you can download from this book's download page (Appendix C) and use with the Excel Guides contain a DATA worksheet that follows the rules of this section. Any of those worksheets can be used as additional models for the method you use to enter variable data in Excel.

EG1.3 OPENING and SAVING WORKBOOKS

You open and save workbooks by first selecting the folder that stores the workbook and then specifying the file name of the workbook. In Excel 2010, you select **File → Open** to open a workbook file or **File → Save As** to save a workbook. In Excel 2007, you select **Office Button → Open** to open a workbook file or **Office Button → Save As** to save a workbook. **Open** and **Save As** display nearly identical dialog boxes that vary only slightly among the different Excel versions. Figure EG1.2 shows the Excel 2010 Open and Save As dialog boxes.

FIGURE EG1.2

Excel 2010 Open and Save As dialog boxes

You select the storage folder by using the drop-down list at the top of either of these dialog boxes. You enter, or select from the list box, a file name for the workbook in the **File name** box. You click **Open** or **Save** to complete the task. Sometimes when saving files, you may want to change the file type before you click **Save**. If you want to save your workbook in the format used by Excel 2003 and earlier versions, select **Excel 97-2003 Workbook (*.xls)** from the **Save as type** drop-down list (shown in Figure EG1.2) before you click **Save**. If you want to save data in a form that can be opened by programs that cannot open Excel workbooks, you might select either **Text (Tab delimited) (*.txt)** or **CSV (Comma delimited) (*.csv)** as the save type.

When you want to open a file and cannot find its name in the list box, double-check that the current **Look in** folder is the folder you intend. If it is, change the file type to **All Files (*.*)** to see all files in the current folder. This technique can help you discover inadvertent misspellings or missing file extensions that otherwise prevent the file from being displayed.

Although all versions of Microsoft Excel include a **Save** command, you should avoid this choice until you gain experience. Using Save makes it too easy to inadvertently overwrite your work. Also, you cannot use the Save command for any open workbook that Excel has marked as read-only. (Use Save As to save such workbooks.)

EG1.4 CREATING and COPYING WORKSHEETS

You create new worksheets by either creating a new workbook or by inserting a new worksheet in an open workbook. To create a new workbook, select **File → New** (Excel 2010) or **Office Button → New** (Excel 2007) and in the pane that appears, double-click the **Blank workbook** icon.

New workbooks are created with a fixed number of worksheets. To delete extra worksheets or insert more sheets, right-click a sheet tab and click either **Delete** or **Insert** (see Figure EG1.3). By default, Excel names a worksheet serially in the form Sheet1, Sheet2, and so on. You should change these names to better reflect the content of your worksheets. To rename a worksheet, double-click the sheet tab of the worksheet, type the new name, and press **Enter**.

FIGURE EG1.3

Sheet tab shortcut menu and the Move or Copy dialog box

You can also make a copy of a worksheet or move a worksheet to another position in the same workbook or to a second workbook. Right-click the sheet tab and select **Move or Copy** from the shortcut menu that appears. In the **To book** drop-down list of the Move or Copy dialog box (see Figure EG1.3), first select **(new book)** (or the name of the pre-existing target workbook), check **Create a copy**, and then click **OK**.

EG1.5 PRINTING WORKSHEETS

To print a worksheet (or a chart sheet), first open to the worksheet by clicking its sheet tab. Then, in Excel 2010, select **File → Print**. If the print preview displayed (see Figure EG1.4) contains errors or displays the worksheet in an undesirable manner, click **File**, make the necessary corrections or adjustments, and repeat **File → Print**. When you are satisfied with the preview, click the large **Print** button.

FIGURE EG1.4

Excel 2010 and Excel 2007 (inset) Print Preview (left) and Page Setup dialog box (right)

In Excel 2007, the same process requires more mouse clicks. First click **Office Button** and then move the mouse pointer over (but do not click) **Print**. In the Preview and Print gallery, click **Print Preview**. If the preview displayed (see Figure EG1.4) contains errors or displays the worksheet in an undesirable manner, click **Close Print Preview**, make the necessary changes, and reselect the print preview. After completing all corrections and adjustments, click **Print** in the Print Preview window to display the Print dialog box (shown in Appendix Section B.3). Select the printer to be used from the **Name** drop-down list, click **All** and **Active sheet(s)**, adjust the **Number of copies**, and click **OK**.

If necessary, you can adjust print formatting while in print preview by clicking the **Page Setup** icon (Excel 2007) or the **Page Setup** link (Excel 2010) to display the Page Setup dialog box (the right panel of Figure EG1.4). For example, to print your worksheet with gridlines and numbered row and lettered column headings (similar to the appearance of the worksheet on-screen), click the **Sheet** tab in the Page Setup dialog box, check **Gridlines** and **Row and column headings**, and click **OK**.

Although every version of Excel offers the (print) **Entire workbook** choice, you get the best results if you print each worksheet separately when you need to print out more than one worksheet (or chart sheet).

EG1.6 WORKSHEET ENTRIES and REFERENCES

When you open to a specific worksheet in a workbook, you use the cursor keys or your pointing device to move a **cell pointer** through the worksheet to select a specific cell for entry. As you type an entry, it appears in the formula bar, and you place that entry in the cell by either pressing the **Tab** key or **Enter** key or clicking the checkmark button in the formula bar.

In worksheets that you use for intermediate calculations or results, you might enter **formulas**, instructions to perform a calculation or some other task, in addition to the numeric and text entries you otherwise make in cells.

Formulas typically use values found in other cells to compute a result that is displayed in the cell that stores the formula. With formulas, the displayed result automatically changes as the dependent values in the other cells change. This process, called **recalculation**, was the original novel feature of spreadsheet programs and led to these programs being widely used in accounting. (Worksheets that contain formulas are sometimes called "live" worksheets to distinguish them from "dead" worksheets—worksheets without any formulas and therefore not capable of recalculation.)

To refer to a cell in a formula, you use a **cell address** in the form *SheetName!ColumnRow*. For example, **Data!A2** refers to the cell in the Data worksheet that is in column A and row 2. You can also use just the *ColumnRow* portion of a full address, for example, **A2**, if you are referring to a cell on the same worksheet as the one into which you are entering a formula. If the sheet name contains spaces or special characters, for example, **CITY DATA** or **Figure_1.2**, you must enclose the sheet name in a pair of single quotes, as in **'CITY DATA'!A2** or **'Figure_1.2'!A2**.

When you want to refer to a group of cells, such as the cells of a column that store the data for a particular variable, you use a **cell range**. A cell range names the upper-leftmost cell and the lower-rightmost cell of the group using the form *SheetName!UpperLeftCell:LowerRightCell*. For example, the cell range **DATA!A1:A11** identifies the first 11 cells in the first column of the **DATA worksheet**. Cell ranges can extend over multiple columns; the cell range **DATA!A1:D11** would refer to the first 11 cells in the first 4 columns of the worksheet.

As with a single cell reference, you can skip the *SheetName!* part of the reference if you are referring to a cell range on the current worksheet and you must use a pair of single quotes if a sheet name contains spaces or special characters. However, in some dialog boxes, you must include the sheet name in a cell reference in order to get the proper results. (In such cases, the instructions in this book include the sheet name; otherwise, they do not.)

Although not used in this book, cell references can include a workbook name in the form **'[WorkbookName] SheetName'!ColumnRow** or **'[WorkbookName] SheetName'! UpperLeft Cell:LowerRightCell.** You might discover such references if you inadvertently copy certain types of worksheets or chart sheets from one workbook to another.

EG1.7 ABSOLUTE and RELATIVE CELL REFERENCES

Many worksheets contain columns (or rows) of similar-looking formulas. For example, column C in a worksheet might contain formulas that sum the contents of the column A and column B rows. The formula for cell C2 would be **=A2 + B2**, the formula for cell C3 would be **=A3 + B3**, for cell C4, **=A4 + B4**, and so on down column C. To avoid the drudgery of typing many similar formulas, you can copy a formula and paste it into all the cells in a selected cell range. For example, to copy a formula that has been entered in cell C2 down the column through row 12:

1. Right-click cell **C2** and click **Copy** from the shortcut menu. A movie marquee–like highlight appears around cell C2.

2. Select the cell range **C3:C12**. (See Appendix B if you need help selecting a cell range.)

3. With the cell range highlighted, right-click over the cell range and click **Paste** from the shortcut menu.

When you perform this copy-and-paste operation, Excel adjusts the cell references in formulas so that copying

the formula **=A2 + B2** from cell C2 to cell C3 results in the formula **=A3 + B3** being pasted into cell C3, the formula **=A4 + B4** being pasted into cell C4, and so on.

There are circumstances in which you do not want Excel to adjust all or part of a formula. For example, if you were copying the cell C2 formula **=(A2 + B2)/B15**, and cell B15 contained the divisor to be used in all formulas, you would not want to see pasted into cell C3 the formula **=(A3 + B3)/B16**. To prevent Excel from adjusting a cell reference, you use an **absolute cell reference** by inserting dollar signs ($) before the column and row references. For example, the absolute cell reference **$B$15** in the copied cell C2 formula **=(A2 + B2)/$B$15** would cause Excel to paste **=(A3 + B3)/$B$15** into cell C3. (For ease of reading, formulas shown in the worksheet illustrations in this book generally do not include absolute cell references.)

Do not confuse the use of the U.S. dollar symbol in an absolute reference with the formatting operation that displays numbers as U.S. currency values.

EG1.8 ENTERING FORMULAS into WORKSHEETS

You enter formulas by typing the equal sign (=) followed by a combination of mathematical and data-processing operations. For simple formulas, you use the symbols +, −, *, /, and ^ for the operations addition, subtraction, multiplication, division, and exponentiation (a number raised to a power), respectively. For example, the formula **=DATA!B2 + DATA!B3 + DATA!B4** adds the contents of cells B2, B3, and B4 of the DATA worksheet and displays the sum as the value in the cell containing the formula.

You can also use **worksheet functions** in formulas to simplify formulas. To use a worksheet function in a formula, either type the function as shown in the instructions in this book or use the Excel Function Wizard feature to insert the function. To use this feature, select **Formulas → Insert Function** and then make the necessary entries and selections in one or more dialog boxes that follow.

If you enter formulas in your worksheets, you should review and verify those formulas before you use their results. To view the formulas in a worksheet, press **Ctrl+`** (grave accent). To restore the original view, the results of the formulas, press **Ctrl+`** a second time. (A "formulas view" accompanies most of the worksheet illustrations in this book.)

EG1.9 USING APPENDICES D and F

Appendices D and F contain additional Excel-related material that you may need to know, depending on how you use this book. If you plan to use PHStat2, make sure you have read Sections D.1 through D.3 in Appendix D. If you would like to learn formatting worksheet details such as how to make the contents of cells appear boldfaced or how to control the number of decimal places displayed, read Sections F.1 and F.2 in Appendix F.

CHAPTER 1 MINITAB GUIDE

MG1.1 GETTING STARTED with MINITAB

You are almost ready to use Minitab if you have completed the Table 1.2 checklist and reviewed the Table 1.3 computing conventions on page 11. Before using Minitab for a specific analysis, you should practice using the Minitab user interface.

Minitab project components appear in separate windows *inside* the Minitab window. In Figure MG1.1 these separate windows have been overlapped, but you can arrange or hide these windows in any way you like. When you start Minitab, you typically see a new project that contains only the session area and one worksheet window. (You can view other components by selecting them in the Minitab **Window** menu.) You can open and save an entire project or, as is done in this book, open and save individual worksheets.

FIGURE MG1.1

Minitab main worksheet with overlapping session, worksheet, chart, and Project Manager windows

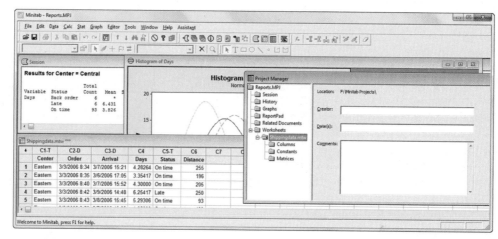

MG1.2 ENTERING DATA and VARIABLE TYPE

As first discussed in Section 1.5, you enter the data for each variable in a separate column. By convention, you start with the first column, initially labeled **C1** by Minitab, and enter the name of each variable into the cells of the unnumbered, shaded first row and then the data for the variable into the numbered rows, as shown in Figure MG1.1.

Minitab infers the variable type from the data you enter in a column. If Minitab discovers a column containing numbers, it treats the column as a numerical variable. If Minitab discovers a column containing words or alphanumeric entries, it treats the column as "text" variable (appropriate for use as a categorical variable). If Minitab discovers a column containing entries that can be interpreted as dates or times, it treats the column as a date/time variable, a special type of numerical variable. This imperfect method works most of the time in Minitab, especially if you make sure that the categories for your categorical variables are words or phrases such as "yes" and "no."

When Minitab identifies a text or date/time variable, it appends a "-T" or "-D" to its column heading for the variable. For example, in Figure MG1.1 above:

- C1-T and C5-T mean that the first and fifth columns contain text variables.
- C2-D and C3-D mean that the second and third columns contain date/time variables.
- C4 and C6 mean that the fourth and sixth columns contain numerical variables.

Because Minitab explicitly defines the variable type, unlike in Excel, your ability to do nonsensical things (such as use a statistical method that is designed for numerical variables on categorical data) is limited. If Minitab misinterprets your data, you can attempt to change the variable type by selecting **Data → Change Data Type** and then selecting the appropriate change from the submenu.

When you enter data, never skip any rows in a column. Minitab interprets skipped rows as missing values. You can use the Minitab workbooks that you can download from this book's download page (see Appendix C) as models for the method you use to enter variable data in Minitab.

MG1.3 OPENING and SAVING WORKSHEETS and PROJECTS

You open and save Minitab worksheet or project files by first selecting the folder that stores a workbook and then specifying the file name of the workbook. To open a worksheet, you select **File → Open Worksheet**. To open a project, you select **File → Open Project**. To save a worksheet, you select **File → Save Current Worksheet As**. To save a project, you select **File → Save Project As**.

Both pairs of open and save commands display nearly identical dialog boxes. Figure MG1.2 shows the Minitab 16 Open Worksheet and Save Current Worksheet As dialog boxes.

FIGURE MG1.2

Minitab 16 Open Worksheet and Save Current Worksheet As dialog boxes

Inside the open or save dialog boxes, you select the storage folder by using the drop-down list at the top of either dialog box. You enter or select from the list box a file name for the workbook in the **File name** box. You click **Open** or **Save** to complete the task. Sometimes when saving files, you might want to change the file type before you click **Save**. If you want to save your data as an Excel worksheet, select **Excel 97-2003** from the **Save as type** drop-down list before you click **Save**. If you want to save data in a form that can be opened by programs that cannot open Excel workbooks, you might select one of the **Text** or **CSV** choices as the **Save as type** type.

When you want to open a file and cannot find its name in the list box, double-check that the current **Look in** folder is the folder you intend. If it is, change the file type to **All (*.*)** to see all files in the current folder. This technique can help you discover inadvertent misspellings or missing file extensions that otherwise prevent the file from being displayed.

When you save a project, you can click **Options** in the Save Project As dialog box and then specify which parts of the project you want to save in a Save Project - Options dialog box (not shown).

Although Minitab includes the **Save Current Worksheet** and **Save Project** commands (commands without the "**As**"), you should avoid this choice until you gain experience. Using Save makes it too easy to inadvertently overwrite your work. Also, you cannot use the Save command for any open workbook that Minitab has marked as read-only. (Use Save As to save such workbooks.)

Individual graphs and a project's session window can also be opened and saved separately in Minitab, although these operations are never used in this book.

MG1.4 CREATING and COPYING WORKSHEETS

You create new worksheets by either creating a new project or by inserting a new worksheet in an open project. To create a new project, select **File ➔ New** and in the New dialog box, click **Minitab Project** and then click **OK**. To insert a new worksheet, also select **File ➔ New** but in the New dialog box click **Minitab Worksheet** and then click **OK**.

A new project is created with one new worksheet. To insert another worksheet, select **File ➔ New** and in the New dialog box click **Minitab Worksheet** and then click **OK**. You can also insert a copy of a worksheet from another project into the current project. Select **File ➔ Open Worksheet** and select the *project* that contains the worksheet to be copied. Selecting a project (and not a worksheet) causes an additional dialog box to be displayed, in which you can specify which worksheets of that second project are to be copied and inserted into the current project.

By default, Minitab names a worksheet serially in the form Worksheet1, Worksheet2, and so on. You should change these names to better reflect the content of your worksheets. To rename a worksheet, open the Project Manager window (see Figure MG1.1), right-click the worksheet name in the left pane, select **Rename** from the shortcut menu, type in the new name, and press **Enter**. You can also use the **Save Current Worksheet As** command discussed in Section MG1.3, although this command also saves the worksheet as a separate file.

MG1.5 PRINTING PARTS of a PROJECT

To print a worksheet, a graph, or the contents of a session, first select the window that corresponds to the object you want to print. Then select **File ➔ Print** *object*, where *object* is either **Worksheet**, **Graph**, or **Session Window**, depending on which object you first selected.

If you are printing a graph or a session window, selecting the **Print** command displays the Print dialog box. The Print dialog box allows you to select the printer to be used, what pages to print, and the number of copies to produce. If you need to change these settings, change them before clicking **OK** to create your printout.

If you are printing a worksheet, selecting **Print Worksheet** displays the Data Window Print Options dialog box (see Figure MG1.3). In this dialog box, you specify the formatting options for your printout (the default selections should be fine), enter a **Title**, and click **OK**. Minitab then presents the Print dialog box discussed in the previous paragraph.

If you need to change the paper size or paper orientation of your printout, select **File ➔ Print Setup** before you select the Print command, make the appropriate selections in the dialog box that appears, and click **OK**.

FIGURE MG1.3
Data Window Print Options dialog box

MG1.6 WORKSHEET ENTRIES and REFERENCES

You refer to individual variables in one of two ways. You can use their column number, such as C1 in Figure MG1.1 on page 21, that appears at the top of a worksheet. Or you can use the variable name that you entered into the cells of the unnumbered, shaded second row, such as Center or Order (in Figure MG1.1). For most statistical analyses, Minitab presents a list of column numbers and their corresponding variable names (if any) from which you make selections. For a variable name such as **Return 2009**, that contains spaces or other special characters, Minitab displays the name using a pair of single quotation marks—for example, **'Return 2009'**—and you need to include those quotation marks any time you type such a variable name in a Minitab dialog box.

For clarity and to minimize errors, this book generally refers to columns by their variable names. In later chapters, you will see that Minitab allows you to refer to several consecutive columns by using a hyphen. For example, either **C1-C6** or **Center-Distance** would refer to all six columns of the Shipping data worksheet shown in Figure MG1.1.

MG1.7 USING APPENDICES D and F

Appendices D and F contain additional Minitab-related material of a general nature. Consult these appendices if you have a question about using Minitab that is not answered in the Minitab Guides of this book.

2 Organizing and Visualizing Data

Learning Objectives

In this chapter, you learn:

- The sources of data used in business
- To construct tables and charts for categorical data
- To construct tables and charts for numerical data
- The principles of properly presenting graphs

©Steve Cole/iStockphoto.com

@ Choice Is Yours, Part I

The Choice Is Yours investment service helps clients with their investment choices. Choice Is Yours evaluates investments as diverse as real estate, direct private equity investments, derivatives, and various specialized types of mutual funds. You've been hired to assist clients who seek to invest in mutual funds, which pool the money of many individual clients and invest the money in a mix of securities and other investments. (To learn more about mutual funds, visit **investopedia.com/university/mutualfunds**.) Because mutual funds that are highly invested in common stocks have had mixed returns recently, Choice Is Yours wants to examine mutual funds that focus on investing in certain types of bonds. Company analysts have selected a sample of 184 such funds that they believe might interest clients. You have been asked to present data about these funds in a way that will help customers make good investment choices. What facts about each bond mutual fund would you collect to help customers compare and contrast the many funds?

A good starting point would be to collect data that would help customers classify mutual funds into various categories. You could research such things as the amount of risk involved in a fund's investment strategy and the type of bonds in which the mutual fund primarily invests. Of course, you would want to learn how well the fund performed in the past, and you would want to supply the customer with several measures of each fund's past performance. (Although past performance is no assurance of future performance, past data could give customers insight into how well each mutual fund has been managed.)

As you further think about your task, you realize that the data for all 184 mutual funds would be a lot for anyone to review. You have been asked to present data about these funds in a way that will help customers make good investment choices. How can you review and explore such data in a comprehensible manner? What facts about each fund would you collect to help customers compare and contrast the many funds?

The challenge you face in Part I of the Choice Is Yours scenario is to examine a large amount of data and reach conclusions based on those data. You can make this business task more manageable by breaking it into these five steps:

- **Define** the variables that you want to study in order to solve a business problem or meet a business objective
- **Collect** the data from appropriate sources
- **Organize** the data collected by developing tables
- **Visualize** the data by developing charts
- **Analyze** the data by examining the appropriate tables and charts (and in later chapters by using other statistical methods) to reach conclusions.

These five steps, known by the acronym **DCOVA** (for **D**efine, **C**ollect, **O**rganize, **V**isualize, and **A**nalyze), are used throughout this book as the basis for statistical problem solving (see Reference 2). In Chapter 1, you already learned that defining a variable includes developing an operational definition and identifying the type of variable. In this chapter, you will learn more about the steps involved in collecting, organizing, visualizing, and analyzing the data.

To help illustrate the DCOVA approach, this chapter frequently uses for its examples the sample of 184 mutual funds that specialize in bond investments mentioned in Part I of the Choice Is Yours scenario. (To examine this sample, open Bond Funds, one of the data files you can download for use with this book as explained in Appendix C.) By the end of the chapter, you will be able to answer the questions posed in the scenario. For example, you will be able to answer questions that compare two categories of bond funds, such as "Is there a difference in the returns of intermediate government bond funds and short-term corporate bond funds?" or "Do intermediate government bond funds tend to be less risky investments than short-term corporate bond funds?"

2.1 Data Collection

Once you have defined your variables, you may need to collect the data for those variables. Examples of **data collection** include the following:

- A marketing analyst who needs to assess the effectiveness of a new television advertisement
- A pharmaceutical manufacturer that needs to determine whether a new drug is more effective than those currently in use
- An operations manager who wants to improve a manufacturing or service process
- An auditor who wants to review the financial transactions of a company in order to determine whether the company is in compliance with generally accepted accounting principles

When you collect data, you use either a **primary data source** or a **secondary data source.** You are using a primary data source when you collect your own data for analysis, and you are using a secondary source if the data for your analysis have been collected by someone else. Data collection often involves collecting data from a sample because collecting data from every item or individual in a population is typically too difficult or too time-consuming. (See Chapter 7 to learn more about sample selection methods.)

Organizations and individuals that collect and publish data often use their data as a primary source and may let others use those data as a secondary source. For example, the U.S. federal government collects and distributes data in this way for both public and private purposes. The Bureau of Labor Statistics collects data on employment and also distributes the monthly consumer price index. The Census Bureau oversees a variety of ongoing surveys regarding population, housing, and manufacturing and undertakes special studies on topics such as crime, travel, and health care.

Data sources are created in one of four ways:

- As data distributed by an organization or individual
- As outcomes of a designed experiment

- As responses from a survey
- As a result of conducting an observational study

Market research companies and trade associations distribute data pertaining to specific industries or markets. Investment services such as Mergent (**www.mergent.com**) provide financial data on a company-by-company basis. Syndicated services such as Nielsen provide clients with data that enables client products to be compared with those of their competitors. On the other hand, daily newspapers are secondary sources that are filled with numerical information regarding stock prices, weather conditions, and sports statistics obtained from primary sources.

Conducting a designed experiment is another source of data. For example, one such experiment might test several laundry detergents to compare how well each detergent removes a certain type of stain. Developing proper experimental designs is a subject mostly beyond the scope of this book because such designs often involve sophisticated statistical procedures. However, some of the fundamental experimental design concepts are discussed in Chapter 10.

Conducting a survey is a third type of data source. People being surveyed are asked questions about their beliefs, attitudes, behaviors, and other characteristics. For example, people could be asked their opinion about which laundry detergent best removes a certain type of stain. (This could lead to a result different from a designed experiment seeking the same answer.) One good way to avoid data-collection flaws when using such a survey is to distribute the questionnaire to a random sample of respondents. (Chapter 7 explains how to collect a random sample.) A bad way would be to rely on a business-rating website that allows online visitors to rate a merchant. Such websites cannot provide assurance that those who do the ratings are representative of the population of customers—or that they even *are* customers.

Conducting an observational study is the fourth data source. A researcher collects data by directly observing a behavior, usually in a natural or neutral setting. Observational studies are a common tool for data collection in business. For example, market researchers use focus groups to elicit unstructured responses to open-ended questions posed by a moderator to a target audience. You can also use observational study techniques to enhance teamwork or improve the quality of products and services.

Problems for Section 2.1

APPLYING THE CONCEPTS

2.1. The Data and Story Library (DASL) is an online library of data files and stories that illustrate the use of basic statistical methods. Visit **lib.stat.cmu.edu/index.php**, click DASL and explore a data set of interest to you. Which of the four sources of data best describes the sources of the data set you selected?

2.2. Visit the website of the Gallup organization, at **www.gallup.com**. Read today's top story. What type of data source is the top story based on?

2.3. A supermarket chain wants to determine the best placement for the supermarket brand of soft drink. What type of data collection source do you think that the supermarket chain should use?

2.4. Visit the "Longitudinal Employer-Household Dynamics" page of the U.S. Census Bureau website, **lehd.did.census.gov/led/**. Examine the "Did You Know" panel on the page. What type of data source is the information presented here based on?

ORGANIZING DATA

After you define your variables and collect your data, you organize your data to help prepare for the later steps of visualizing and analyzing your data. The techniques you use to organize your data depend on the type of variable (categorical or numerical) associated with your data.

2.2 Organizing Categorical Data

Starting with this section, the sections of the Excel and Minitab Guides duplicate the sections in the main chapter. For example, to learn how to use Excel or Minitab to organize categorical data, see either Section EG2.2 or MG2.2.

You organize categorical data by tallying responses by categories and placing the results in tables. Typically, you construct a summary table to organize the data for a single categorical variable and you construct a contingency table to organize the data from two or more categorical variables.

The Summary Table

A **summary table** presents tallied responses as frequencies or percentages for each category. A summary table helps you see the differences among the categories by displaying the frequency, amount, or percentage of items in a set of categories in a separate column. Table 2.1 shows a summary table (stored in `Bill Payment`) that tallies the responses to a recent survey that asked adults how they pay their monthly bills.

TABLE 2.1

Types of Bill Payment

Form of Payment	Percentage (%)
Cash	15
Check	54
Electronic/online	28
Other/don't know	3

Source: *Data extracted from "How Adults Pay Monthly Bills,"* USA Today, *October 4, 2007, p. 1.*

From Table 2.1, you can conclude that more than half the people pay by check and 82% pay by either check or by electronic/online forms of payment.

EXAMPLE 2.1

Summary Table of Levels of Risk of Bond Funds

The 184 bond funds involved in Part I of the Choice Is Yours scenario (see page 25) are classified according to their risk level, categorized as below average, average, and above average. Construct a summary table of the bond funds, categorized by risk.

SOLUTION From Table 2.2, you can see that about the same number of funds are below average, average, and above average in risk. This means that 69.57% of the bond funds are classified as having an average or above average level of risk.

TABLE 2.2

Frequency and Percentage Summary Table Pertaining to Risk Level for 184 Bond Funds

Fund Risk Level	Number of Funds	Percentage of Funds (%)
Below average	56	30.43%
Average	69	37.50%
Above average	59	32.07%
Total	184	100.00%

The Contingency Table

A **contingency table** allows you to study patterns that may exist between the responses of two or more categorical variables. This type of table cross-tabulates, or tallies jointly, the responses of the categorical variables. In the simplest case of two categorical variables, the joint responses appear in a table such that the category tallies of one variable are located in the rows and the category tallies of the other variable are located in the columns. Intersections of the rows and columns are called **cells**, and each cell contains a value associated with a unique pair of responses for the two variables (e.g., Fee: Yes and Type: Intermediate Government in Table 2.3). Cells can contain the frequency, the percentage of the overall total, the percentage of the row total, or the percentage of the column total, depending on the type of contingency table being used.

In Part I of the Choice Is Yours scenario, you could create a contingency table to examine whether there is any pattern between the type of bond fund (intermediate government or short-term corporate) and whether the fund charges a fee (yes or no). You would begin by tallying the joint responses for each of the mutual funds in the sample of 184 bond mutual funds (stored in Bond Funds). You tally a response into one of the four possible cells in the table, depending on the type of bond fund and whether the fund charges a fee. For example, the first fund listed in the sample is classified as an intermediate government fund that does not charge a fee. Therefore, you tally this joint response into the cell that is the intersection of the Intermediate Government row and the No column. Table 2.3 shows the completed contingency table after all 184 bond funds have been tallied.

TABLE 2.3

Contingency Table Displaying Type of Fund and Whether a Fee Is Charged

TYPE	FEE		
	Yes	No	Total
Intermediate government	34	53	87
Short-term corporate	20	77	97
Total	54	130	184

To look for other patterns between the type of bond fund and whether the fund charges a fee, you can construct contingency tables that show cell values as a percentage of the overall total (the 184 mutual funds), the row totals (the 87 intermediate government funds and the 97 short-term corporate bond funds), and the column totals (the 54 funds that charge a fee and the 130 funds that do not charge a fee). Tables 2.4, 2.5, and 2.6 present these contingency tables.

Table 2.4 shows that 47.28% of the bond funds sampled are intermediate government funds, 52.72% are short-term corporate bond funds, and 18.48% are intermediate

TABLE 2.4

Contingency Table Displaying Type of Fund and Whether a Fee Is Charged, Based on Percentage of Overall Total

TYPE	FEE		
	Yes	No	Total
Intermediate government	18.48	28.80	47.28
Short-term corporate	10.87	41.85	52.72
Total	29.35	70.65	100.00

government funds that charge a fee. Table 2.5 shows that 39.08% of the intermediate government funds charge a fee, while 20.62% of the short-term corporate bond funds charge

TABLE 2.5

Contingency Table Displaying Type of Fund and Whether a Fee Is Charged, Based on Percentage of Row Total

TYPE	FEE		
	Yes	No	Total
Intermediate government	39.08	60.92	100.00
Short-term corporate	20.62	79.38	100.00
Total	29.35	70.65	100.00

a fee. Table 2.6 shows that of the funds that charge a fee, 62.96% are intermediate government funds. From the tables, you see that intermediate government funds are much more likely to charge a fee.

TABLE 2.6

Contingency Table Displaying Type of Fund and Whether a Fee Is Charged, Based on Percentage of Column Total

	FEE		
TYPE	**Yes**	**No**	**Total**
Intermediate government	62.96	40.77	47.28
Short-term corporate	37.04	59.23	52.72
Total	100.00	100.00	100.00

Problems for Section 2.2

LEARNING THE BASICS

2.5 A categorical variable has three categories, with the following frequencies of occurrence:

Category	Frequency
A	13
B	28
C	9

a. Compute the percentage of values in each category.
b. What conclusions can you reach concerning the categories?

2.6 The following data represent the responses to two questions asked in a survey of 40 college students majoring in business: What is your gender? (M = male; F = female) and What is your major? (A = Accounting; C = Computer Information Systems; M = Marketing):

a. Tally the data into a contingency table where the two rows represent the gender categories and the three columns represent the academic major categories.
b. Construct contingency tables based on percentages of all 40 student responses, based on row percentages and based on column percentages.

Gender:	M	M	M	F	M	F	F	M	F	M	F	M	M	M	M	F	F	M	F	F
Major:	A	C	C	M	A	C	A	A	C	C	A	A	A	M	C	M	A	A	A	C
Gender:	M	M	M	M	F	M	F	F	M	M	F	M	M	M	M	F	M	F	M	M
Major:	C	C	A	A	M	M	M	C	A	A	A	C	C	A	A	A	C	C	A	C

APPLYING THE CONCEPTS

2.7 The Transportation Security Administration reported that from January 1, 2008, to February 18, 2009, more than 14,000 banned items were collected at Palm Beach International Airport. The categories were as follows:

Category	Frequency
Flammables/irritants	8,350
Knives and blades	4,134
Prohibited tools	753
Sharp objects	497
Other	357

a. Compute the percentage of values in each category.
b. What conclusions can you reach concerning the banned items?

 2.8 The following table represents world oil consumption in millions of barrels a day in 2009:

Region	Oil Consumption (millions of barrels a day)
Developed Europe	14.5
Japan	4.4
United States	18.8
Rest of the world	46.7

Source: Energy Information Administration, 2009.

a. Compute the percentage of values in each category.
b. What conclusions can you reach concerning the consumption of oil in 2009?

2.9 Federal obligations for benefit programs and the national debt were \$63.8 trillion in 2008. The cost per household (\$) for various categories was as follows:

Category	Cost per Household (\$)
Civil servant retirement	15,851
Federal debt	54,537
Medicare	284,288
Military retirement	29,694
Social Security	160,216
Other	2,172

Source: Data extracted from "What We Owe," *USA Today,* May 29, 2009, p. 1A.

a. Compute the percentage of values in each category.
b. What conclusions can you reach concerning the benefit programs?

2.10 A survey of 1,085 adults asked "Do you enjoy shopping for clothing for yourself?" The results (data extracted from "Split decision on clothes shopping," *USA Today*, January 28, 2011, p. 1B) indicated that 51% of the females enjoyed shopping for clothing for themselves as compared to 44% of the males. The sample sizes of males and females was not provided. Suppose that the results were as shown in the following table: are summarized in the following table:

ENJOY SHOPPING FOR CLOTHING FOR YOURSELF	GENDER		
	Male	Female	Total
Yes	238	276	514
No	304	267	571
Total	542	543	1,085

a. Construct contingency tables based on total percentages, row percentages, and column percentages.
b. What conclusions do you reach from these analyses?

2.11 Each day at a large hospital, several hundred laboratory tests are performed. The rate at which these tests are done improperly (and therefore need to be redone) seems steady, at about 4%. In an effort to get to the root cause of these nonconformances, tests that need to be redone, the director of the lab decided to keep records over a period of one week. The laboratory tests were subdivided by the shift of workers who performed the lab tests. The results are as follows:

LAB TESTS PERFORMED	SHIFT		
	Day	Evening	Total
Nonconforming	16	24	40
Conforming	654	306	960
Total	670	330	1,000

a. Construct contingency tables based on total percentages, row percentages, and column percentages.
b. Which type of percentage—row, column, or total—do you think is most informative for these data? Explain.
c. What conclusions concerning the pattern of nonconforming laboratory tests can the laboratory director reach?

2.12 Does it take more time to get yourself removed from an email list than it used to? A study of 100 large online retailers revealed the following:

	NEED THREE OR MORE CLICKS TO BE REMOVED	
YEAR	Yes	No
2009	39	61
2008	7	93

Source: Data extracted from "Drill Down," *The New York Times,* March 29, 2010, p. B2.

What do these results tell you about whether more online retailers were requiring three or more clicks in 2009 than in 2008?

2.3 Organizing Numerical Data

You organize numerical data by creating ordered arrays or distributions. The amount of data you have and what you seek to discover about your variables influences which methods you choose, as does the arrangement of data in your worksheet.

Stacked and Unstacked Data

In Section 1.5, you learned to enter variables into worksheets by columns. When organizing numerical data, you must additionally consider if you will need to analyze a numerical variable by subgroups that are defined by the values of a categorical variable.

For example, in Bond Funds you might want to analyze the numerical variable **Return 2009**, the year 2009 percentage return of a bond fund, by the two subgroups that are defined by the categorical variable **Type**, intermediate government and short-term corporate. To perform this type of subgroup analysis, you arrange your worksheet data either in stacked format or unstacked format, depending on the requirements of the statistical application you plan to use.

In Bond Funds, the data has been entered in **stacked** format, in which the all of the values for a numerical variable appear in one column and a second, separate column contains the categorical values that identify which subgroup the numerical values belong to. For example, all values for the **Return 2009** variable are in one column (the sixth column) and the values in the second column (for the **Type** variable) would be used to determine which of the two **Type** subgroups an individual **Return 2009** value belongs to.

In **unstacked** format, the values for each subgroup of a numerical variable are segregated and placed in separate columns. For example, Return 2009 Unstacked contains the **IG_Return_2009** and **STC_Return_2009** variable columns that contain the data of **Return 2009** in unstacked format by the two subgroups defined by **Type,** intermediate government (IG) and short-term corporate (STC).

While you can always manually stack or unstack your data, Minitab and PHStat2 both provide you with commands that automate these operations. If you use Excel without PHStat2, you *must* use a manual procedure.

The Ordered Array

An **ordered array** arranges the values of a numerical variable in rank order, from the smallest value to the largest value. An ordered array helps you get a better sense of the range of values in your data and is particularly useful when you have more than a few values. For example, Table 2.7A shows the data collected for a study of the cost of meals at 50 restaurants located in a major city and at 50 restaurants located in that city's suburbs (stored in Restaurants). The unordered data in Table 2.7A prevent you from reaching any quick conclusions about the cost of meals.

None of the data sets used in the examples found in the Excel and Minitab Guides require that you stack (or unstack) data. However, you may need to stack (or unstack) data to solve some of the problems in this book.

TABLE 2.7A

Cost per Person at 50 City Restaurants and 50 Suburban Restaurants

City Restaurant Meal Cost									
62	67	23	79	32	38	46	43	39	43
44	29	59	56	32	56	23	40	45	44
40	33	57	43	49	28	35	79	42	21
40	49	45	54	64	48	41	34	53	27
44	58	68	59	61	59	48	78	65	42

Suburban Restaurant Meal Cost									
53	45	39	43	44	29	37	34	33	37
54	30	49	44	34	55	48	36	29	40
38	38	55	43	33	44	41	45	41	42
37	56	60	46	31	35	68	40	51	32
28	44	26	42	37	63	37	22	53	62

In contrast, Table 2.7B, the ordered array version of the same data, enables you to quickly see that the cost of a meal at the city restaurants is between $21 and $79 and that the cost of a meal at the suburban restaurants is between $22 and $68.

When you have a data set that contains a large number of values, reaching conclusions from an ordered array can be difficult. For such data sets, creating a frequency or percentage distribution and a cumulative percentage distribution (see following sections) would be a better choice.

TABLE 2.7B

Ordered Arrays of Cost per Person at 50 City Restaurants and 50 Suburban Restaurants

City Restaurant Meal Cost									
21	23	23	27	28	29	32	32	33	34
35	38	39	40	40	40	41	42	42	43
43	43	44	44	44	45	45	46	48	48
49	49	53	54	56	56	57	58	59	59
59	61	62	64	65	67	68	78	79	79

Suburban Restaurant Meal Cost									
22	26	28	29	29	30	31	32	33	33
34	34	35	36	37	37	37	37	37	38
38	39	40	40	41	41	42	42	43	43
44	44	44	44	45	45	46	48	49	51
53	53	54	55	55	56	60	62	63	68

The Frequency Distribution

A **frequency distribution** summarizes numerical values by tallying them into a set of numerically ordered **classes**. Classes are groups that represent a range of values, called a **class interval**. Each value can be in only one class and every value must be contained in one of the classes.

To create a useful frequency distribution, you must think about how many classes are appropriate for your data and also determine a suitable *width* for each class interval. In general, a frequency distribution should have at least 5 classes but no more than 15 classes because having too few or too many classes provides little new information. To determine the **class interval width** (see Equation 2.1), you subtract the lowest value from the highest value and divide that result by the number of classes you want your frequency distribution to have.

DETERMINING THE CLASS INTERVAL WIDTH

$$\text{Interval width} = \frac{\text{highest value} - \text{lowest value}}{\text{number of classes}} \tag{2.1}$$

Because the city restaurant data consist of a sample of only 50 restaurants, between 5 and 10 classes are acceptable. From the ordered city cost array in Table 2.7B, the difference between the highest value of $79 and the lowest value of $21 is $58. Using Equation (2.1), you approximate the class interval width as follows:

$$\text{Interval width} = \frac{58}{10} = 5.8$$

This result suggests that you should choose an interval width of $5.80. However, your width should always be an amount that simplifies the reading and interpretation of the frequency distribution. In this example, an interval width of $10 would be much better than an interval width of $5.80.

Because each value can appear in only one class, you must establish proper and clearly defined **class boundaries** for each class. For example, if you chose $10 as the class interval for the restaurant data, you would need to establish boundaries that would include all the values and simplify the reading and interpretation of the frequency distribution. Because the cost of a city restaurant meal varies from $21 to $79, establishing the first class interval as from $20 to less than $30, the second from $30 to less than $40, and so on, until the last class interval is from $70 to less than $80, would meet the requirements. Table 2.8 contains frequency distributions of the cost per meal for the 50 city restaurants and the 50 suburban restaurants using these class intervals.

TABLE 2.8

Frequency Distributions of the Cost per Meal for 50 City Restaurants and 50 Suburban Restaurants

Cost per Meal ($)	City Frequency	Suburban Frequency
20 but less than 30	6	5
30 but less than 40	7	17
40 but less than 50	19	17
50 but less than 60	9	7
60 but less than 70	6	4
70 but less than 80	3	0
Total	50	50

The frequency distribution allows you to reach conclusions about the major characteristics of the data. For example, Table 2.8 shows that the cost of meals at city restaurants is concentrated between $40 and $50, while for suburban restaurants the cost of meals is concentrated between $30 and $50.

For some charts discussed later in this chapter, class intervals are identified by their **class midpoints**, the values that are halfway between the lower and upper boundaries of each class. For the frequency distributions shown in Table 2.8, the class midpoints are $25, $35, $45, $55, $65, and $75 (amounts that are simple to read and interpret).

If a data set does not contain a large number of values, different sets of class intervals can create different impressions of the data. Such perceived changes will diminish as you collect more data. Likewise, choosing different lower and upper class boundaries can also affect impressions.

EXAMPLE 2.2

Frequency Distributions of the 2009 Return for Intermediate Government and Short-Term Corporate Bond Mutual Funds

In the Using Statistics scenario, you are interested in comparing the 2009 return of intermediate government and short-term corporate bond mutual funds. Construct frequency distributions for the intermediate government funds and the short-term corporate bond funds.

SOLUTION The 2009 returns of the intermediate government bond funds are highly concentrated between 0 and 10, whereas the 2009 returns of the short-term corporate bond funds are highly concentrated between 5 and 15 (see Table 2.9).

For the bond fund data, the number of *values* is different in the two groups. When the number of *values* in the two groups is not the same, you need to use proportions or relative frequencies and percentages in order to compare the groups.

TABLE 2.9

Frequency Distributions of the 2009 Return for Intermediate Government and Short-Term Corporate Bond Funds

2009 Return	Intermediate Government Frequency	Short-Term Corporate Frequency
−10 but less than −5	0	1
−5 but less than 0	13	0
0 but less than 5	35	15
5 but less than 10	30	38
10 but less than 15	6	31
15 but less than 20	1	9
20 but less than 25	1	1
25 but less than 30	1	1
30 but less than 35	0	1
Total	87	97

The Relative Frequency Distribution and the Percentage Distribution

When you are comparing two or more groups, as is done in Table 2.10, knowing the proportion or percentage of the total that is in each group is more useful than knowing the frequency count of each group. For such situations, you create a relative frequency distribution or a percentage distribution instead of a frequency distribution. (If your two or more groups have different sample sizes as in Example 2.2, you *must* use either a relative frequency distribution or a percentage distribution.)

TABLE 2.10

Relative Frequency Distributions and Percentage Distributions of the Cost of Meals at City and Suburban Restaurants

COST PER MEAL ($)	CITY		SUBURBAN	
	Relative Frequency	Percentage (%)	Relative Frequency	Percentage (%)
20 but less than 30	0.12	12.0	0.10	10.0
30 but less than 40	0.14	14.0	0.34	34.0
40 but less than 50	0.38	38.0	0.34	34.0
50 but less than 60	0.18	18.0	0.14	14.0
60 but less than 70	0.12	12.0	0.08	8.0
70 but less than 80	0.06	6.0	0.00	0.0
Total	1.00	100.0	1.00	100.0

The **proportion**, or **relative frequency**, in each group is equal to the number of *values* in each class divided by the total number of values. The percentage in each group is its proportion multiplied by 100%.

COMPUTING THE PROPORTION OR RELATIVE FREQUENCY

The proportion, or relative frequency, is the number of *values* in each class divided by the total number of values:

$$\text{Proportion} = \text{relative frequency} = \frac{\text{number of values in each class}}{\text{total number of values}} \qquad (2.2)$$

If there are 80 values and the frequency in a certain class is 20, the proportion of values in that class is

$$\frac{20}{80} = 0.25$$

and the percentage is

$$0.25 \times 100\% = 25\%$$

You form the **relative frequency distribution** by first determining the relative frequency in each class. For example, in Table 2.8 on page 34, there are 50 city restaurants, and the cost per meal at 9 of these restaurants is between $50 and $60. Therefore, as shown in Table 2.10, the proportion (or relative frequency) of meals that cost between $50 and $60 at city restaurants is

$$\frac{9}{50} = 0.18$$

You form the **percentage distribution** by multiplying each proportion (or relative frequency) by 100%. Thus, the proportion of meals at city restaurants that cost between $50 and $60 is 9 divided by 50, or 0.18, and the percentage is 18%. Table 2.10 presents the relative frequency distribution and percentage distribution of the cost of meals at city and suburban restaurants.

From Table 2.10, you conclude that meals cost slightly more at city restaurants than at suburban restaurants. Also, 12% of the meals cost between $60 and $70 at city restaurants as compared to 8% of the meals at suburban restaurants; and 14% of the meals cost between $30 and $40 at city restaurants as compared to 34% of the meals at suburban restaurants.

EXAMPLE 2.3

Relative Frequency Distributions and Percentage Distributions of the 2009 Return for Intermediate Government and Short-Term Corporate Bond Mutual Funds

In the Using Statistics scenario, you are interested in comparing the 2009 return of intermediate government and short-term corporate bond mutual funds. Construct relative frequency distributions and percentage distributions for these funds.

SOLUTION You conclude (see Table 2.11) that the 2009 return for the corporate bond funds is much higher than for the intermediate government funds. For example, 31.96% of the corporate bond funds have returns between 10 and 15, while 6.90% of the intermediate government funds have returns between 10 and 15. Of the corporate bond funds, only 15.46% have returns between 0 and 5 as compared to 40.23% of the intermediate government funds.

TABLE 2.11

Relative Frequency Distributions and Percentage Distributions of the 2009 Return for Intermediate Government and Short-Term Corporate Bond Mutual Funds

2009 RETURN	INTERMEDIATE GOVERNMENT		SHORT-TERM CORPORATE	
	Proportion	Percentage	Proportion	Percentage
−10 but less than −5	0.0000	0.00	0.0103	1.03
−5 but less than 0	0.1494	14.94	0.0000	0.00
0 but less than 5	0.4023	40.23	0.1546	15.46
5 but less than 10	0.3448	34.48	0.3918	39.18
10 but less than 15	0.0690	6.90	0.3196	31.96
15 but less than 20	0.0115	1.15	0.0928	9.28
20 but less than 25	0.0115	1.15	0.0103	1.03
25 but less than 30	0.0115	1.15	0.0103	1.03
30 but less than 35	0.0000	0.00	0.0103	1.03
Total	1.0000	100.00	1.0000	100.00

The Cumulative Distribution

The **cumulative percentage distribution** provides a way of presenting information about the percentage of values that are less than a specific amount. For example, you might want to know what percentage of the city restaurant meals cost less than $40 or what percentage cost less than $50. You use the percentage distribution to form the cumulative percentage distribution. Table 2.12 shows how percentages of individual class intervals are combined to form the cumulative percentage distribution for the cost of meals at city restaurants. From this table, you see that none (0%) of the meals cost less than $20, 12% of meals cost less than $30, 26% of meals cost less than $40 (because 14% of the meals cost between $30 and $40), and so on, until all 100% of the meals cost less than $80.

Table 2.13 summarizes the cumulative percentages of the cost of city and suburban restaurant meals. The cumulative distribution shows that the cost of meals is slightly lower in suburban restaurants than in city restaurants. Table 2.13 shows that 44% of the meals at suburban restaurants cost less than $40 as compared to 26% of the meals at city restaurants; 78% of the

TABLE 2.12

Developing the Cumulative Percentage Distribution for the Cost of Meals at City Restaurants

Cost per Meal ($)	Percentage (%)	Percentage of Meals Less Than Lower Boundary of Class Interval (%)
20 but less than 30	12	0
30 but less than 40	14	12
40 but less than 50	38	26 = 12 + 14
50 but less than 60	18	64 = 12 + 14 + 38
60 but less than 70	12	82 = 12 + 14 + 38 + 18
70 but less than 80	6	94 = 12 + 14 + 38 + 18 + 12
80 but less than 90	0	100 = 12 + 14 + 38 + 18 + 12 + 6

meals at suburban restaurants cost less than $50 as compared to 64% of the meals at city restaurants; and 92% of the meals at suburban restaurants cost less than $60 as compared to 82% of the meals at city restaurants.

TABLE 2.13

Cumulative Percentage Distributions of the Cost of City and Suburban Restaurant Meals

Cost ($)	Percentage of City Restaurants With Meals Less Than Indicated Amount	Percentage of Suburban Restaurants With Meals Less Than Indicated Amount
20	0	0
30	12	10
40	26	44
50	64	78
60	82	92
70	94	100
80	100	100

EXAMPLE 2.4

Cumulative Percentage Distributions of the 2009 Return for Intermediate Government and Short-Term Corporate Bond Mutual Funds

In the Using Statistics scenario, you are interested in comparing the 2009 return for intermediate government and short-term corporate bond mutual funds. Construct cumulative percentage distributions for the intermediate government and short-term corporate bond mutual funds.

SOLUTION The cumulative distribution in Table 2.14 indicates that returns are much lower for the intermediate government bond funds than for the short-term corporate funds. The table shows that 14.94% of the intermediate government funds have negative returns as compared to 1.03% of the short-term corporate bond funds; 55.17% of the intermediate government funds have returns below 5 as compared to 16.49% of the short-term corporate bond funds; and 89.65% of the intermediate government funds have returns below 10 as compared to 55.67% of the short-term corporate bond funds.

TABLE 2.14

Cumulative Percentage Distributions of the 2009 Return for Intermediate Government and Short-Term Corporate Bond Funds

2009 Return	Intermediate Government Percentage Less Than Indicated Value	Short-Term Corporate Percentage Less Than Indicated Value
−10	0.00	0.00
−5	0.00	1.03
0	14.94	1.03
5	55.17	16.49
10	89.65	55.67
15	96.55	87.63
20	97.70	96.91
25	98.85	97.94
30	100.00	98.97
35	100.00	100.00

Problems for Section 2.3

LEARNING THE BASICS

2.13 Construct an ordered array, given the following data from a sample of $n = 7$ midterm exam scores in accounting:

68   94   63   75   71   88   64

2.14 Construct an ordered array, given the following data from a sample of midterm exam scores in marketing:

88   78   78   73   91   78   85

2.15 The GMAT scores from a sample of 50 applicants to an MBA program indicate that none of the applicants scored below 450. A frequency distribution was formed by choosing class intervals 450 to 499, 500 to 549, and so on, with the last class having an interval from 700 to 749. Two applicants scored in the interval 450 to 499, and 16 applicants scored in the interval 500 to 549.

a. What percentage of applicants scored below 500?
b. What percentage of applicants scored between 500 and 549?
c. What percentage of applicants scored below 550?
d. What percentage of applicants scored below 750?

2.16 A set of data has values that vary from 11.6 to 97.8.

a. If these values are grouped into nine classes, indicate the class boundaries.
b. What class interval width did you choose?
c. What are the nine class midpoints?

APPLYING THE CONCEPTS

2.17 The file **BBCost 2010** contains the total cost ($) for four tickets, two beers, four soft drinks, four hot dogs, two game programs, two baseball caps, and parking for one vehicle at each of the 30 Major League Baseball parks during the 2010 season. These costs were

172,335,250,180,173,162,132,207,316,178,184,141,168,208,115

158,330,151,161,170,212,222,160,227,227,127,217,121,221,216

Source: Data extracted from **teammarketing.com**, April 1, 2010.

a. Organize these costs as an ordered array.
b. Construct a frequency distribution and a percentage distribution for these costs.
c. Around which class grouping, if any, are the costs of attending a baseball game concentrated? Explain.

✓ SELF Test 2.18 The file **Utility** contains the data in the next column about the cost of electricity during July 2011 for a random sample of 50 one-bedroom apartments in a large city.

a. Construct a frequency distribution and a percentage distribution that have class intervals with the upper class boundaries $99, $119, and so on.
b. Construct a cumulative percentage distribution.

c. Around what amount does the monthly electricity cost seem to be concentrated?

Raw Data on Utility Charges ($)

96	171	202	178	147	102	153	197	127	82
157	185	90	116	172	111	148	213	130	165
141	149	206	175	123	128	144	168	109	167
95	163	150	154	130	143	187	166	139	149
108	119	183	151	114	135	191	137	129	158

2.19 One operation of a mill is to cut pieces of steel into parts that will later be used as the frame for front seats in an automobile. The steel is cut with a diamond saw and requires the resulting parts to be within ±0.005 inch of the length specified by the automobile company. Data are collected from a sample of 100 steel parts and stored in **Steel**. The measurement reported is the difference in inches between the actual length of the steel part, as measured by a laser measurement device, and the specified length of the steel part. For example, the first value, −0.002, represents a steel part that is 0.002 inch shorter than the specified length.

a. Construct a frequency distribution and a percentage distribution.
b. Construct a cumulative percentage distribution.
c. Is the steel mill doing a good job meeting the requirements set by the automobile company? Explain.

2.20 A manufacturing company produces steel housings for electrical equipment. The main component part of the housing is a steel trough that is made out of a 14-gauge steel coil. It is produced using a 250-ton progressive punch press with a wipe-down operation that puts two 90-degree forms in the flat steel to make the trough. The distance from one side of the form to the other is critical because of weatherproofing in outdoor applications. The company requires that the width of the trough be between 8.31 inches and 8.61 inches. The widths of the troughs, in inches, are collected from a sample of 49 troughs and stored in **Trough** and shown here:

8.312	8.343	8.317	8.383	8.348	8.410	8.351	8.373
8.481	8.422	8.476	8.382	8.484	8.403	8.414	8.419
8.385	8.465	8.498	8.447	8.436	8.413	8.489	8.414
8.481	8.415	8.479	8.429	8.458	8.462	8.460	8.444
8.429	8.460	8.412	8.420	8.410	8.405	8.323	8.420
8.396	8.447	8.405	8.439	8.411	8.427	8.420	8.498
8.409							

a. Construct a frequency distribution and a percentage distribution.
b. Construct a cumulative percentage distribution.
c. What can you conclude about the number of troughs that will meet the company's requirements of troughs being between 8.31 and 8.61 inches wide?

2.21 The manufacturing company in Problem 2.20 also produces electric insulators. If the insulators break when in use, a short circuit is likely to occur. To test the strength of the insulators, destructive testing in high-powered labs is carried out to determine how much *force* is required to break the insulators. Force is measured by observing how many pounds must be applied to the insulator before it breaks. Force measurements are collected from a sample of 30 insulators and stored in Force and shown here:

1,870	1,728	1,656	1,610	1,634	1,784	1,522	1,696
1,592	1,662	1,866	1,764	1,734	1,662	1,734	1,774
1,550	1,756	1,762	1,866	1,820	1,744	1,788	1,688
1,810	1,752	1,680	1,810	1,652	1,736		

a. Construct a frequency distribution and a percentage distribution.
b. Construct a cumulative percentage distribution.
c. What can you conclude about the strength of the insulators if the company requires a force measurement of at least 1,500 pounds before the insulator breaks?

2.22 The file Bulbs contains the life (in hours) of a sample of 40 100-watt light bulbs produced by Manufacturer A and a sample of 40 100-watt light bulbs produced by Manufacturer B. The following table shows these data as a pair of ordered arrays:

Manufacturer A					Manufacturer B				
684	697	720	773	821	819	836	888	897	903
831	835	848	852	852	907	912	918	942	943
859	860	868	870	876	952	959	962	986	992
893	899	905	909	911	994	1,004	1,005	1,007	1,015
922	924	926	926	938	1,016	1,018	1,020	1,022	1,034
939	943	946	954	971	1,038	1,072	1,077	1,077	1,082
972	977	984	1,005	1,014	1,096	1,100	1,113	1,113	1,116
1,016	1,041	1,052	1,080	1,093	1,153	1,154	1,174	1,188	1,230

a. Construct a frequency distribution and a percentage distribution for each manufacturer, using the following class interval widths for each distribution:

Manufacturer A: 650 but less than 750, 750 but less than 850, and so on.
Manufacturer B: 750 but less than 850, 850 but less than 950, and so on.

b. Construct cumulative percentage distributions.
c. Which bulbs have a longer life—those from Manufacturer A or Manufacturer B? Explain.

2.23 The following data (stored in Drink) represent the amount of soft drink in a sample of 50 2-liter bottles:

2.109	2.086	2.066	2.075	2.065	2.057	2.052	2.044	2.036	2.038
2.031	2.029	2.025	2.029	2.023	2.020	2.015	2.014	2.013	2.014
2.012	2.012	2.012	2.010	2.005	2.003	1.999	1.996	1.997	1.992
1.994	1.986	1.984	1.981	1.973	1.975	1.971	1.969	1.966	1.967
1.963	1.957	1.951	1.951	1.947	1.941	1.941	1.938	1.908	1.894

a. Construct a cumulative percentage distribution.
b. On the basis of the results of (a), does the amount of soft drink filled in the bottles concentrate around specific values?

VISUALIZING DATA

When you organize your data, you sometimes begin to discover patterns or relationships in your data, as examples in Sections 2.2 and 2.3 illustrate. To better explore and discover patterns and relationships, you can visualize your data by creating various charts and special "displays." As is the case when organizing data, the techniques you use to visualize your data depend on the *type of* variable (categorical or numerical) contained in your data.

2.4 Visualizing Categorical Data

The chart you choose to visualize the data for a single categorical variable depends on whether you seek to emphasize how categories directly compare to each other (bar chart) or how categories form parts of a whole (pie chart), or whether you have data that are concentrated in only a few of your categories (Pareto chart). To visualize the data for two categorical variables, you use a side-by-side bar chart.

The Bar Chart

A **bar chart** compares different categories by using individual bars to represent the tallies for each category. The length of a bar represents the amount, frequency, or percentage of values falling into a category. Unlike with a histogram, discussed in Section 2.5, a bar chart separates the bars between the categories. Figure 2.1 displays the bar chart for the data of Table 2.1 on page 28, which is based on a recent survey that asked adults how they pay their monthly bills ("How Adults Pay Monthly Bills," *USA Today*, October 4, 2007, p. 1).

FIGURE 2.1

Bar chart for how adults pay their monthly bills

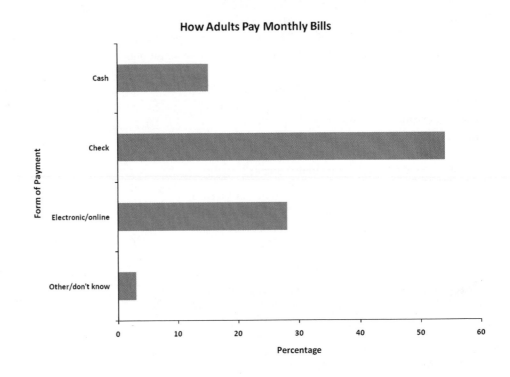

Reviewing Figure 2.1, you see that respondents are most likely to pay by check or electronically/online, followed by paying by cash. Very few respondents mentioned other or did not know.

EXAMPLE 2.5	In Part I of the Choice Is Yours scenario, you are interested in examining the risk of the bond funds. You have already defined the variables and collected the data from a sample of 184 bond funds. Now, you need to construct a bar chart of the risk of the bond funds (based on Table 2.2 on page 28) and interpret the results.
Bar Chart of Levels of Risk of Bond Mutual Funds	**SOLUTION** Reviewing Figure 2.2, you see that average is the largest category, closely followed by above average, and below average.

FIGURE 2.2

Bar chart of the levels of risk of bond mutual funds

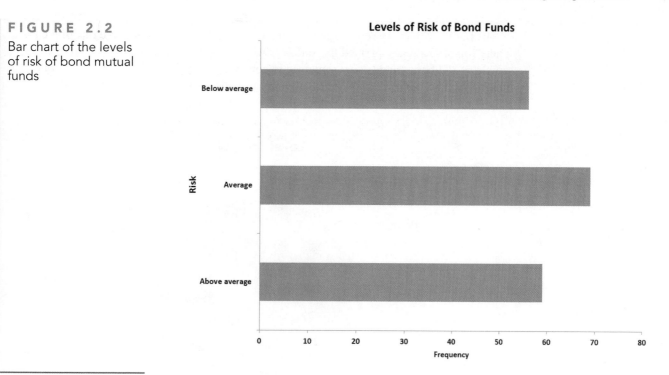

The Pie Chart

A **pie chart** uses parts of a circle to represent the tallies of each category. The size of each part, or pie slice, varies according to the percentage in each category. For example, in Table 2.1 on page 28, 54% of the respondents stated that they paid bills by check. To represent this category as a pie slice, you multiply 54% by the 360 degrees that makes up a circle to get a pie slice that takes up 194.4 degrees of the 360 degrees of the circle. From Figure 2.3, you can see that the pie chart lets you visualize the portion of the entire pie that is in each category. In this figure, paying bills by check is the largest slice, containing 54% of the pie. The second largest slice is paying bills electronically/online, which contains 28% of the pie.

FIGURE 2.3

Pie chart for how people pay their bills

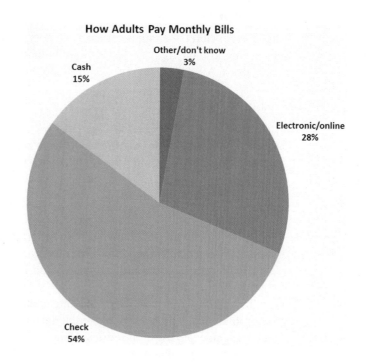

EXAMPLE 2.6

Pie Chart of Levels of Risk of Bond Mutual Funds

FIGURE 2.4

Pie chart of the levels of risk of bond mutual funds

Figure 2.4 shows a pie chart created using Minitab; Figure 2.3 shows a pie chart created using Excel.

In Part I of the Choice Is Yours scenario, you are interested in examining the risk of the bond funds. You have already defined the variables to be collected and collected the data from a sample of 184 bond funds. Now, you need to construct a pie chart of the risk of the bond funds (based on Table 2.2 on page 28) and interpret the results.

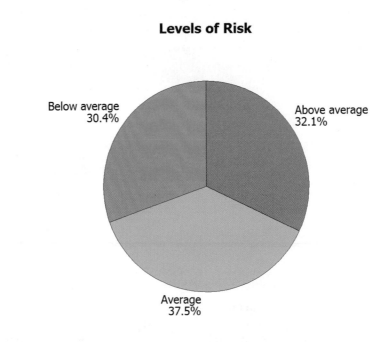

Levels of Risk

SOLUTION   Reviewing Figure 2.4, you see that approximately a little more than one-third of the funds are average risk, about one-third are above average risk, and fewer than one-third are below-average risk.

The Pareto Chart

In a **Pareto chart**, the tallies for each category are plotted as vertical bars in descending order, according to their frequencies, and are combined with a cumulative percentage line on the same chart. A Pareto chart can reveal situations in which the Pareto principle occurs.

> PARETO PRINCIPLE
>
> The **Pareto principle** exists when the majority of items in a set of data occur in a small number of categories and the few remaining items are spread out over a large number of categories. These two groups are often referred to as the "vital few" and the "trivial many."

A Pareto chart has the capability to separate the "vital few" from the "trivial many," enabling you to focus on the important categories. In situations in which the data involved consist of defective or nonconforming items, a Pareto chart is a powerful tool for prioritizing improvement efforts.

To study a situation in which the Pareto chart proved to be especially appropriate, consider the problem faced by a bank. The bank defined the problem to be the incomplete automated teller machine (ATM) transactions. Data concerning the causes of incomplete ATM transactions were collected and stored in **ATM Transactions** . Table 2.15 shows the causes of incomplete ATM transactions, the frequency for each cause, and the percentage of incomplete ATM transactions due to each cause.

TABLE 2.15

Summary Table of
Causes of Incomplete
ATM Transactions

Cause	Frequency	Percentage (%)
ATM malfunctions	32	4.42
ATM out of cash	28	3.87
Invalid amount requested	23	3.18
Lack of funds in account	19	2.62
Magnetic strip unreadable	234	32.32
Warped card jammed	365	50.41
Wrong key stroke	23	3.18
Total	724	100.00

Source: Data extracted from A. Bhalla, "Don't Misuse the Pareto Principle,"
Six Sigma Forum Magazine, May 2009, pp. 15–18.

Table 2.16 presents a summary table for the incomplete ATM transactions data in which the categories are ordered based on the frequency of incomplete ATM transactions present (rather than arranged alphabetically). The percentages and cumulative percentages for the ordered categories are also included as part of the table.

TABLE 2.16

Ordered Summary Table
of Causes of Incomplete
ATM Transactions

Cause	Frequency	Percentage (%)	Cumulative Percentage (%)
Warped card jammed	365	50.41%	50.41%
Magnetic strip unreadable	234	32.32%	82.73%
ATM malfunctions	32	4.42%	87.15%
ATM out of cash	28	3.87%	91.02%
Invalid amount requested	23	3.18%	94.20%
Wrong key stroke	23	3.18%	97.38%
Lack of funds in account	19	2.62%	100.00%
Total	724	100.00%	

Figure 2.5 shows a Pareto chart based on the results displayed in Table 2.16.

FIGURE 2.5

Pareto chart for the
incomplete ATM
transactions data

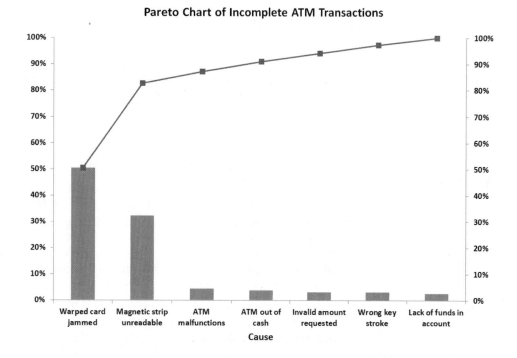

Pareto Chart of Incomplete ATM Transactions

A Pareto chart presents the bars vertically, along with a cumulative percentage line. The cumulative line is plotted at the midpoint of each category, at a height equal to the cumulative percentage. In order for a Pareto chart to include all categories, even those with few defects, in some situations, you need to include a category labeled *Other* or *Miscellaneous*. In these situations, the bar representing these categories should be placed to the right of the other bars.

Because the categories in a Pareto chart are ordered by the frequency of occurrence, you can see where to concentrate efforts to improve the process. Analyzing the Pareto chart in Figure 2.5, if you follow the line, you see that these first two categories account for 82.73% of the incomplete ATM transactions. The first category listed is warped card jammed (with 50.41% of the defects), followed by magnetic strip unreadable (with 32.32%). Attempts to reduce incomplete ATM transactions due to warped card jammed and magnetic strip unreadable should produce the greatest payoff. The team should focus on finding why these errors occurred.

EXAMPLE 2.7

Pareto Chart of Types of Bill Payment

FIGURE 2.6

Pareto chart of bill payment

Figure 2.6 shows a Pareto chart created using Minitab; Figure 2.5 shows a Pareto chart created using Excel.

Construct a Pareto chart of the types of bill payment (see Table 2.1 on page 28)

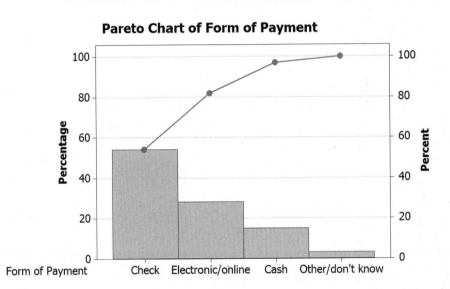

Pareto Chart of Form of Payment

In Figure 2.6, check and electronic/online account for 82% of the bill payments and check, electronic/online, and cash account for 97% of the bill payments.

The Side-by-Side Bar Chart

A **side-by-side bar chart** uses sets of bars to show the joint responses from two categorical variables. Figure 2.7 uses the data of Table 2.3 on page 29, which shows the frequency of bond funds that charge a fee for the intermediate government bond funds and short-term corporate bond funds.

Reviewing Figure 2.7, you see that a much higher number of the intermediate government bond funds charge a fee than the short-term corporate bond funds.

FIGURE 2.7
Side-by-side bar chart of fund type and whether a fee is charged

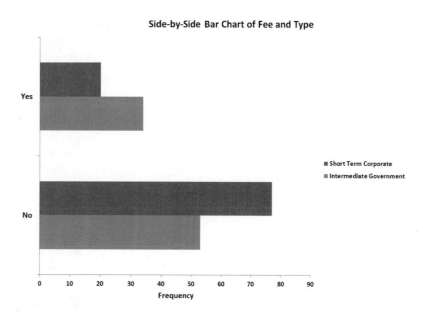

Side-by-Side Bar Chart of Fee and Type

■ Short Term Corporate
■ Intermediate Government

Frequency

Problems for Section 2.4

APPLYING THE CONCEPTS

SELF Test **2.24** A survey asked 1,264 women who were their most trusted shopping advisers. The survey results were as follows:

Shopping Advisers	Percentage (%)
Advertising	7
Friends/family	45
Manufacturer websites	5
News media	11
Online user reviews	13
Retail websites	4
Salespeople	1
Other	14

Source: Data extracted from "Snapshots," *USA Today,* October 19, 2006, p. 1B.

a. Construct a bar chart, a pie chart, and a Pareto chart.
b. Which graphical method do you think is best for portraying these data?
c. What conclusions can you reach concerning women's most trusted shopping advisers?

2.25 What do college students do with their time? A survey of 3,000 traditional-age students was taken with the results shown at the top of the next column.
a. Construct a bar chart, a pie chart, and a Pareto chart.
b. Which graphical method do you think is best for portraying these data?

c. What conclusions can you reach concerning what college students do with their time?

Activity	Percentage (%)
Attending class/lab	9
Sleeping	24
Socializing, recreating, other	51
Studying	7
Working, volunteering, student clubs	9

Source: Data extracted from M. Marklein, "First Two years of College Wasted?" *USA Today,* January 18, 2011, p. 3A.

2.26 The Energy Information Administration reported the following sources of electricity in the United States in 2010:

Source of Electricity	Percentage (%)
Coal	44
Hydroelectric	7
Natural gas	24
Nuclear	20
Other	5

Source: Energy Information Administration, 2010.

a. Construct a Pareto chart.

b. What percentage of power is derived from coal, nuclear, or natural gas?

c. Construct a pie chart.

d. For these data, do you prefer using a Pareto chart or the pie chart? Why?

2.27 An article discussed radiation therapy and new cures from the therapy, along with the harm that could be done if mistakes were made. The following tables represent the results of the types of mistakes made and the causes of mistakes reported to the New York State Department of Health from 2001 to 2009:

Radiation Mistakes	Number
Missed all or part of intended target	284
Wrong dose given	255
Wrong patient treated	50
Other	32

a. Construct a bar chart and a pie chart for the types of radiation mistakes.

b. Which graphical method do you think is best for portraying these data?

Causes of Mistakes	Number
Quality assurance flawed	355
Data entry or calculation errors by personnel	252
Misidentification of patient or treatment location	174
Blocks, wedges, or collimators misused	133
Patient's physical setup wrong	96
Treatment plan flawed	77
Hardware malfunction	60
Staffing	52
Computer software or digital information transfer malfunction	24
Override of computer data by personnel	19
Miscommunication	14
Unclear/other	8

Source: Data extracted from W. Bogdanich, "A Lifesaving Tool Turned Deadly," *The New York Times*, January 24, 2010, pp. 1, 15, 16.

c. Construct a Pareto chart for the causes of mistakes.

d. Discuss the "vital few" and "trivial many" reasons for the causes of mistakes.

2.28 The following table indicates the percentage of residential electricity consumption in the United States, organized by type of appliance in a recent year:

Type of Appliance	Percentage (%)
Air conditioning	18
Clothes dryers	5
Clothes washers/other	24
Computers	1
Cooking	2
Dishwashers	2
Freezers	2
Lighting	16
Refrigeration	9
Space heating	7
Water heating	8
TVs and set top boxes	6

Source: Data extracted from J. Mouawad, and K. Galbraith, "Plugged-in Age Feeds a Hunger for Electricity," *The New York Times*, September 20, 2009, pp. 1, 28.

a. Construct a bar chart, a pie chart, and a Pareto chart.

b. Which graphical method do you think is best for portraying these data?

c. What conclusions can you reach concerning residential electricity consumption in the United States?

2.29 A study of 1,000 people asked what respondents wanted to grill during barbecue season. The results were as follows:

Type of Food	Percentage (%)
Beef	38
Chicken	23
Fruit	1
Hot dogs	6
Pork	8
Seafood	19
Vegetables	5

Source: Data extracted from "What Folks Want Sizzling on the Grill During Barbecue Season," *USA Today*, March 29, 2009, p. 1A.

a. Construct a bar chart, a pie chart, and a Pareto chart.

b. Which graphical method do you think is best for portraying these data?

c. What conclusions can you reach concerning what folks want sizzling on the grill during barbecue season?

2.30 A survey of 1,085 adults asked "Do you enjoy shopping for clothing for yourself?" The results (data extracted from "Split decision on clothes shopping," *USA Today*, January 28, 2011, p. 1B) indicated that 51% of the females enjoyed shopping for clothing for themselves as compared to 44% of the males. The sample sizes of males and females was not provided. Suppose that the results were as shown in the following table:

ENJOY SHOPPING FOR CLOTHING	GENDER		
	Male	Female	Total
Yes	238	276	514
No	304	267	571
Total	542	543	1,085

a. Construct a side-by-side bar chart of enjoying shopping and gender.
b. What conclusions do you reach from this chart?

2.31 Each day at a large hospital, several hundred laboratory tests are performed. The rate at which these tests are done improperly (and therefore need to be redone) seems steady, at about 4%. In an effort to get to the root cause of these nonconformances, tests that need to be redone, the director of the lab decided to keep records over a period of one week. The laboratory tests were subdivided by the shift of workers who performed the lab tests. The results are as follows:

LAB TESTS PERFORMED	SHIFT		
	Day	Evening	Total
Nonconforming	16	24	40
Conforming	654	306	960
Total	670	330	1,000

a. Construct a side-by-side bar chart of nonconformances and shift.
b. What conclusions concerning the pattern of nonconforming laboratory tests can the laboratory director reach?

2.32 Does it take more time to get yourself removed from an email list than it used to? A study of 100 large online retailers revealed the following:

YEAR	NEED THREE OR MORE CLICKS TO BE REMOVED	
	Yes	No
2009	39	61
2008	7	93

Source: Data extracted from "Drill Down," *The New York Times,* March 29, 2010, p. B2.

a. Construct a side-by-side bar chart of year and whether you need to click three or more times to be removed from an email list.
b. What do these results tell you about whether more online retailers were requiring three or more clicks in 2009 than in 2008?

2.5 Visualizing Numerical Data

Among the charts you use to visualize numerical data are the stem-and-leaf display, the histogram, the percentage polygon, and the cumulative percentage polygon (ogive).

The Stem-and-Leaf Display

A **stem-and-leaf display** allows you to see how the data are distributed and where concentrations of data exist. The display organizes data into groups (the stems) row-wise, so that the values within each group (the leaves) branch out to the right of their stem. On each leaf, the values are presented in ascending order. For example, suppose you collect the following lunch costs ($) for 15 classmates who had lunch at a fast-food restaurant:

5.40 4.30 4.80 5.50 7.30 8.50 6.10 4.80 4.90 4.90 5.50 3.50 5.90 6.30 6.60

To construct the stem-and-leaf display, you use whole dollar amounts as the stems and round the cents, the leaves, to one decimal place. For the first value, 5.40, the stem would be 5 and its leaf would be 4. For the second value, 4.30, the stem would be 4 and its leaf 3. The completed stem-and-leaf display for these data is

```
3 | 5
4 | 38899
5 | 4559
6 | 136
7 | 3
8 | 5
```

EXAMPLE 2.8

Stem-and-Leaf Display of the 2009 Return of the Short-Term Corporate Bond Funds

FIGURE 2.8

Stem-and-leaf display of the return in 2009 of short-term corporate bond funds

Figure 2.8 shows a stem-and-leaf display created using Minitab and modified so that each stem occupies only one row. The leaves using PHStat2 will differ from Figure 2.8 slightly because PHStat2 and Minitab use different methods.

In Part I of the Choice Is Yours scenario, you are interested in studying the past performance of the short-term corporate bond funds. One measure of past performance is the return in 2009. You have already defined the variables to be collected and collected the data from a sample of 97 short-term corporate bond funds. Now, you need to construct a stem-and-leaf display of the return in 2009.

SOLUTION Figure 2.8 illustrates the stem-and-leaf display of the return in 2009 for short-term corporate bond funds.

```
Stem-and-Leaf Display: Return 2009_Short Term Corporat

Stem-and-leaf of Return 2009_Short Term Corporat   N  = 97
Leaf Unit = 1.0

   1    -0  8
 (53)    0  11222223334444455555555566666666677777788888889999999
  43     1  000000111111222222233333333334445555566679
   3     2  4
   2     2  9
   1     3  2
```

Analyzing Figure 2.8, you conclude the following:

- The lowest return in 2009 was –8.
- The highest return in 2009 was 32.
- The returns in 2009 were concentrated between 0 and 20.
- Only one fund had a negative 2009 return, and three funds had 2009 returns 20 and above.

The Histogram

A **histogram** is a bar chart for grouped numerical data in which you use vertical bars to represent the frequencies or percentages in each group. In a histogram, there are no gaps between adjacent bars. You display the variable of interest along the horizontal (X) axis. The vertical (Y) axis represents either the frequency or the percentage of values per class interval.

Figure 2.9 displays frequency histograms for the cost of meals at city restaurants and suburban restaurants. The histogram for city restaurants shows that the cost of meals is concentrated between approximately $40 and $50. Very few meals at city restaurants cost more than

FIGURE 2.9

Histograms for the cost of restaurant meals at city and suburban restaurants

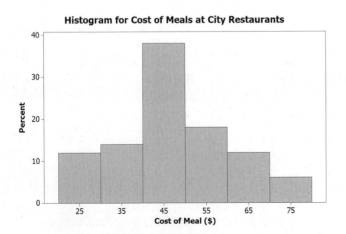
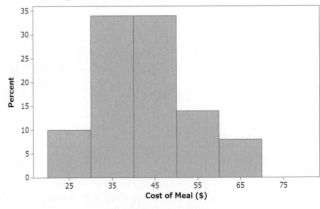

$70. The histogram for suburban restaurants shows that the cost of meals is concentrated between $30 and $50. Very few meals at suburban restaurants cost more than $60.

EXAMPLE 2.9

Histograms of the 2009 Return for the Intermediate Government and Short-Term Corporate Bond Funds

In Part I of the Choice Is Yours scenario, you are interested in comparing the past performance of the intermediate government bond funds and the short-term corporate bond funds. One measure of past performance is the return in 2009. You have already defined the variables to be collected and collected the data from a sample of 184 bond funds. Now, you need to construct histograms for the intermediate government and the short-term corporate bond funds.

SOLUTION Figure 2.10 displays frequency histograms for the 2009 return for the intermediate government and short-term corporate bond funds.

FIGURE 2.10

Frequency histograms of the 2009 return for the intermediate government and short-term corporate bond funds

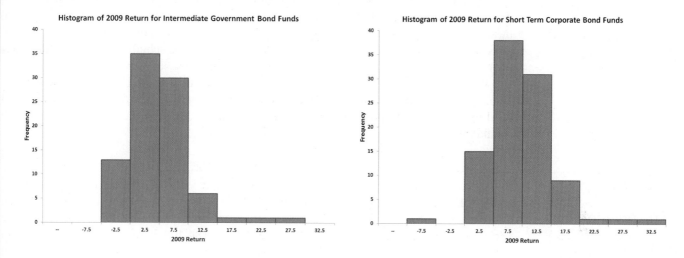

Figure 2.10 shows histograms created using Excel and PHStat2; Figure 2.9 shows histograms created using Minitab.

Reviewing the histograms in Figure 2.10 leads you to conclude that the returns were much higher for the short-term corporate bond funds than for the intermediate government bond funds. The return for intermediate government bond funds is concentrated between 0 and 10, and the return for the short-term corporate bond funds is concentrated between 5 and 15.

The Percentage Polygon

If you tried to construct two or more histograms on the same graph, you would not be able to easily interpret each histogram because the bars would overlap. When there are two or more groups, you should use a percentage polygon. A **percentage polygon** uses the midpoints of each class interval to represent the data of each class and then plots the midpoints, at their respective class percentages, as points on a line.

Figure 2.11 displays percentage polygons for the cost of meals at city and suburban restaurants.

Reviewing the two polygons in Figure 2.11 leads you to conclude that the highest concentration of the cost of meals at city restaurants is between $40 and $50, while the cost of meals at suburban restaurants is evenly concentrated between $30 and $50. Also, city restaurants have a higher percentage of meals that cost $60 or more than suburban restaurants.

FIGURE 2.11
Percentage polygons of the cost of restaurant meals for city and suburban restaurants

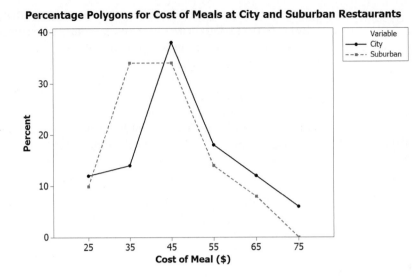

The polygons in Figure 2.11 have points whose values on the X axis represent the midpoint of the class interval. For example, look at the points plotted at $X = 65$ ($65). The point for the cost of meals at city restaurants (the higher one) represents the fact that 12% of the meals at these restaurants cost between $60 and $70. The point for the cost of meals at suburban restaurants (the lower one) represents the fact that 8% of meals at these restaurants cost between $60 and $70.

When you construct polygons or histograms, the vertical (Y) axis should show the true zero, or "origin," so as not to distort the character of the data. The horizontal (X) axis does not need to show the zero point for the variable of interest, although the range of the variable should include the major portion of the axis.

EXAMPLE 2.10

Percentage Polygons of the 2009 Return for the Intermediate Government and Short-Term Corporate Bond Funds

In Part I of the Choice Is Yours scenario, you are interested in comparing the past performance of the intermediate government bond funds and the short-term corporate bond funds. One measure of past performance is the return in 2009. You have already defined the variables and collected the data from a sample of 184 bond funds. Now, you need to construct percentage polygons for the intermediate government bond and short-term corporate bond funds.

SOLUTION Figure 2.12 displays percentage polygons of the 2009 returns for the intermediate government bond and short-term corporate bond funds.

FIGURE 2.12

Percentage polygons of the 2009 return for the intermediate government bond and short-term corporate bond funds

Figure 2.12 shows percentage polygons created using Excel; Figure 2.11 shows percentage polygons created using Minitab.

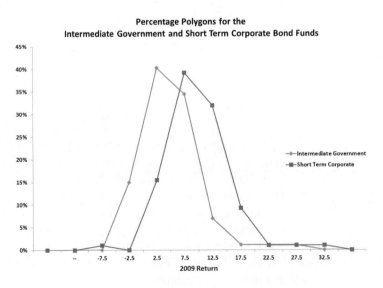

Analyzing Figure 2.12 leads you to conclude that the 2009 return of short-term corporate funds is much higher than for intermediate government bond funds. The polygon for the short-term corporate funds is to the right (the returns are higher) of the polygon for the intermediate government bond funds. The return for intermediate government funds is concentrated between 0 and 10, whereas the return for the short-term corporate bond funds is concentrated between 5 and 15.

The Cumulative Percentage Polygon (Ogive)

The **cumulative percentage polygon**, or **ogive**, uses the cumulative percentage distribution discussed in Section 2.3 to display the variable of interest along the X axis and the cumulative percentages along the Y axis.

Figure 2.13 shows cumulative percentage polygons for the cost of meals at city and suburban restaurants.

FIGURE 2.13

Cumulative percentage polygons of the cost of restaurant meals at city and suburban restaurants

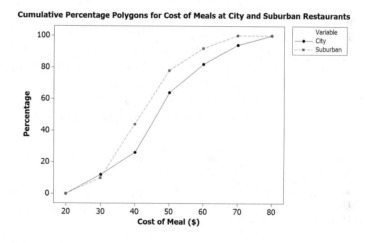

Reviewing the curves leads you to conclude that the curve of the cost of meals at the city restaurants is located to the right of the curve for the suburban restaurants. This indicates that the city restaurants have fewer meals that cost less than a particular value. For example, 64% of the meals at city restaurants cost less than $50, as compared to 78% of the meals at suburban restaurants.

EXAMPLE 2.11

Cumulative Percentage Polygons of the 2009 Return for the Intermediate Government and Short-Term Corporate Bond Funds

In Part I of the Choice Is Yours scenario, you are interested in comparing the past performance of the intermediate government bond funds and the short-term corporate bond funds. One measure of past performance is the return in 2009. You have already defined the variables and collected the data from a sample of 184 bond funds. Now, you need to construct cumulative percentage polygons for the intermediate government bond and the short-term corporate bond funds.

SOLUTION Figure 2.14 on page 52 displays cumulative percentage polygons for the 2009 return for the intermediate government bond and short-term corporate bond funds.

FIGURE 2.14

Cumulative percentage polygons of the 2009 return of intermediate government bonds and short-term corporate bond funds

Figure 2.14 shows cumulative percentage polygons created using Excel; Figure 2.13 shows cumulative percentage polygons created using Minitab.

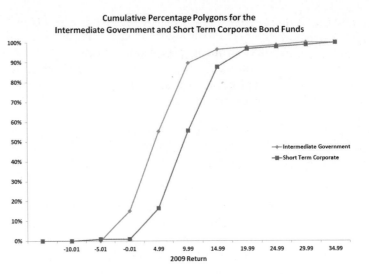

Reviewing the cumulative percentage polygons in Figure 2.14 leads you to conclude that the curve for the 2009 return of short-term corporate bond funds is located to the right of the curve for the intermediate government bond funds. This indicates that the short-term corporate bond funds have fewer 2009 returns that are lower than a particular value. For example, 14.94% of the intermediate government bond funds had negative (returns below 0) 2009 returns as compared to only 1.03% of the short-term corporate bond funds. Also, 55.17% of the intermediate government bond funds had 2009 returns below 5, as compared to 16.49% of the short-term corporate bond funds. You can conclude that, in general, the short-term corporate bond funds outperformed the intermediate government bond funds in 2009.

Problems for Section 2.5

LEARNING THE BASICS

2.33 Construct a stem-and-leaf display, given the following data from a sample of midterm exam scores in finance:

54   69   98   93   53   74

2.34 Construct an ordered array, given the following stem-and-leaf display from a sample of $n = 7$ midterm exam scores in information systems:

```
5 | 0
6 |
7 | 446
8 | 19
9 | 2
```

APPLYING THE CONCEPTS

2.35 The following is a stem-and-leaf display representing the amount of gasoline purchased, in gallons (with leaves in tenths of gallons), for a sample of 25 cars that use a particular service station on the New Jersey Turnpike:

```
 9 | 147
10 | 02238
11 | 125566777
12 | 223489
13 | 02
```

a. Construct an ordered array.
b. Which of these two displays seems to provide more information? Discuss.
c. What amount of gasoline (in gallons) is most likely to be purchased?
d. Is there a concentration of the purchase amounts in the center of the distribution?

✓ SELF Test **2.36** The file **BBCost 2010** contains the total cost ($) for four tickets, two beers, four soft drinks, four hot dogs, two game programs, two baseball caps, and parking for one vehicle at each of the 30 Major League Baseball parks during the 2010 season.

Source: Data extracted from **teammarketing.com,** April 1, 2010.

a. Construct a stem-and-leaf display for these data.
b. Around what value, if any, are the costs of attending a baseball game concentrated? Explain.

2.37 The file **DarkChocolate** contains the cost per ounce ($) for a sample of 14 dark chocolate bars:

| 0.68 | 0.72 | 0.92 | 1.14 | 1.42 | 0.94 | 0.77 |
| 0.57 | 1.51 | 0.57 | 0.55 | 0.86 | 1.41 | 0.90 |

Source: Data extracted from "Dark Chocolate: Which Bars Are Best?" *Consumer Reports*, September 2007, p. 8.

a. Construct an ordered array.

b. Construct a stem-and-leaf display.

c. Does the ordered array or the stem-and-leaf display provide more information? Discuss.

d. Around what value, if any, is the cost of dark chocolate bars concentrated? Explain.

2.38 The file `Utility` contains the following data about the cost of electricity during July 2011 for a random sample of 50 one-bedroom apartments in a large city:

96	171	202	178	147	102	153	197	127	82
157	185	90	116	172	111	148	213	130	165
141	149	206	175	123	128	144	168	109	167
95	163	150	154	130	143	187	166	139	149
108	119	183	151	114	135	191	137	129	158

a. Construct a histogram and a percentage polygon.

b. Construct a cumulative percentage polygon.

c. Around what amount does the monthly electricity cost seem to be concentrated?

2.39 As player salaries have increased, the cost of attending baseball games has increased dramatically. The following histogram visualizes the total cost ($) for four tickets, two beers, four soft drinks, four hot dogs, two game programs, two baseball caps, and parking for one vehicle at each of the 30 Major League Baseball parks during the 2009 season that is stored in `BBCost 2009`.

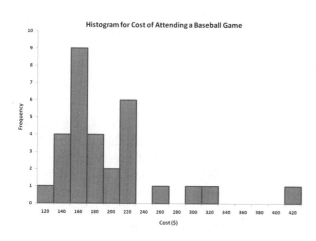

What conclusions can you reach concerning the cost of attending a baseball game at different ballparks?

2.40 The following histogram visualizes the data about the property taxes per capita for the 50 states and the District of Columbia, stored in `PropertyTaxes`.

What conclusions can you reach concerning the property taxes per capita?

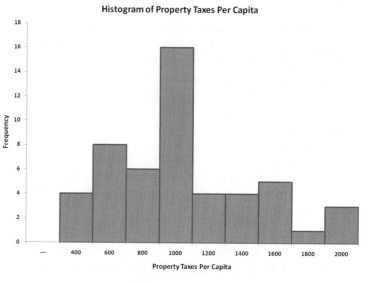

2.41 One operation of a mill is to cut pieces of steel into parts that will later be used as the frame for front seats in an automobile. The steel is cut with a diamond saw and requires the resulting parts to be within ±0.005 inch of the length specified by the automobile company. The data are collected from a sample of 100 steel parts and stored in `Steel`. The measurement reported is the difference in inches between the actual length of the steel part, as measured by a laser measurement device, and the specified length of the steel part. For example, the first value, −0.002, represents a steel part that is 0.002 inch shorter than the specified length.

a. Construct a percentage histogram.

b. Is the steel mill doing a good job meeting the requirements set by the automobile company? Explain.

2.42 A manufacturing company produces steel housings for electrical equipment. The main component part of the housing is a steel trough that is made out of a 14-gauge steel coil. It is produced using a 250-ton progressive punch press with a wipe-down operation that puts two 90-degree forms in the flat steel to make the trough. The distance from one side of the form to the other is critical because of weatherproofing in outdoor applications. The company requires that the width of the trough be between 8.31 inches and 8.61 inches. The widths of the troughs, in inches, are collected from a sample of 49 troughs and stored in `Trough`.

a. Construct a percentage histogram and a percentage polygon.

b. Plot a cumulative percentage polygon.

c. What can you conclude about the number of troughs that will meet the company's requirements of troughs being between 8.31 and 8.61 inches wide?

2.43 The manufacturing company in Problem 2.42 also produces electric insulators. If the insulators break when in use, a short circuit is likely to occur. To test the strength of the insulators, destructive testing in high-powered labs is carried out to determine how much *force* is required to break the insulators. Force is measured by observing how many pounds must be applied to the insulator before it breaks. Force measurements are collected from a sample of 30 insulators and stored in Force .

a. Construct a percentage histogram and a percentage polygon.

b. Construct a cumulative percentage polygon.

c. What can you conclude about the strengths of the insulators if the company requires a force measurement of at least 1,500 pounds before the insulator breaks?

2.44 The file Bulbs contains the life (in hours) of a sample of 40 100-watt light bulbs produced by Manufacturer A and a sample of 40 100-watt light bulbs produced by Manufacturer B. The table in the next column shows these data as a pair of ordered arrays:

Use the following class interval widths for each distribution:

Manufacturer A: 650 but less than 750, 750 but less than 850, and so on.

Manufacturer B: 750 but less than 850, 850 but less than 950, and so on.

Manufacturer A					Manufacturer B				
684	697	720	773	821	819	836	888	897	903
831	835	848	852	852	907	912	918	942	943
859	860	868	870	876	952	959	962	986	992
893	899	905	909	911	994	1,004	1,005	1,007	1,015
922	924	926	926	938	1,016	1,018	1,020	1,022	1,034
939	943	946	954	971	1,038	1,072	1,077	1,077	1,082
972	977	984	1,005	1,014	1,096	1,100	1,113	1,113	1,116
1,016	1,041	1,052	1,080	1,093	1,153	1,154	1,174	1,188	1,230

a. Construct percentage histograms on separate graphs and plot the percentage polygons on one graph.

b. Plot cumulative percentage polygons on one graph.

c. Which manufacturer has bulbs with a longer life—Manufacturer A or Manufacturer B? Explain.

2.45 The data stored in Drink represents the amount of soft drink in a sample of 50 2-liter bottles:

a. Construct a histogram and a percentage polygon.

b. Construct a cumulative percentage polygon.

c. On the basis of the results in (a) and (b), does the amount of soft drink filled in the bottles concentrate around specific values?

2.6 Visualizing Two Numerical Variables

Often you will want to explore possible relationships between two numerical variables. You use a scatter plot as a first step to visualize such relationships. In the special case where one of your variables represents the passage of time, you use a time-series plot.

The Scatter Plot

Often, you have two numerical measurements about the same item or individual. A **scatter plot** can explore the possible relationship between those measurements by plotting the data of one numerical variable on the horizontal, or X, axis and the data of a second numerical variable on the vertical, or Y, axis. For example, a marketing analyst could study the effectiveness of advertising by comparing advertising expenses and sales revenues of 50 stores. Using a scatter plot, a point is plotted on the two-dimensional graph for each store, using the X axis to represent advertising expenses and the Y axis to represent sales revenues.

Table 2.17 presents the revenues and value (both in millions of dollars) for all 30 NBA professional basketball teams that is stored in NBAValues . To explore the possible relationship between the revenues generated by a team and the value of a team, you can create a scatter plot.

TABLE 2.17

Values and Revenues for NBA Teams

Team	Value	Revenues	Team	Value	Revenues
Atlanta	306	103	Milwaukee	254	91
Boston	433	144	Minnesota	268	96
Charlotte	278	96	New Jersey	269	92
Chicago	511	168	New Orleans	267	95
Cleveland	476	159	New York	586	202
Dallas	446	154	Oklahoma City	310	111
Denver	321	115	Orlando	361	107
Detroit	479	171	Philadelphia	344	115
Golden State	315	113	Phoenix	429	148
Houston	470	160	Portland	338	121
Indiana	281	97	Sacramento	305	109
Los Angeles Clippers	295	102	San Antonio	398	133
Los Angeles Lakers	607	209	Toronto	386	133
Memphis	257	88	Utah	343	118
Miami	364	126	Washington	313	110

Source: Data extracted from **www.forbes.com/lists/2009/32/basketball-values-09_NBA-Team-Valuations_Rank.html**.

For each team, you plot the revenues on the X axis and the values on the Y axis. Figure 2.15 presents a scatter plot for these two variables.

FIGURE 2.15

Scatter plot of revenue and value

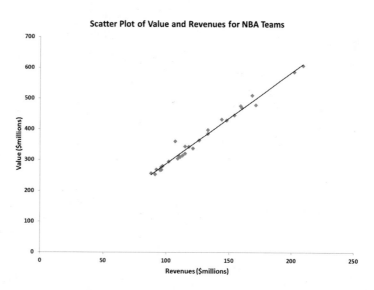

Reviewing Figure 2.15, you see that there appears to be a very strong increasing (positive) relationship between revenues and the value of a team. In other words, teams that generate a smaller amount of revenues have a lower value, while teams that generate higher revenues have a higher value. Notice the straight line that has been superimposed on the plotted data in Figure 2.15. For these data, this line is very close to the points in the scatter plot. This line is a linear regression prediction line that will be discussed in Chapter 12. (In Section 3.5, you will return to this example when you learn about the covariance and the coefficient of correlation.)

Other pairs of variables may have a decreasing (negative) relationship in which one variable decreases as the other increases. In other situations, there may be a weak or no relationship between the variables.

The Time-Series Plot

A **time-series plot** plots the values of a numerical variable on the Y axis and plots the time period associated with each numerical value on the X axis. A time-series plot can help explore trends in data that occur over time. For example, Table 2.18 presents the combined gross (in millions of dollars) of movies released from 1996 to 2009 that is stored in MovieGross. To better visualize this data, you create the time-series plot shown in Figure 2.16.

From Figure 2.16, you see that there was a steady increase in the combined gross of movies between 1996 and 2009. During that time, the combined gross increased from under $6 billion in 1996 to more than $10 billion in 2009.

TABLE 2.18

Combined Gross of Movies

Year	Combined Gross
1996	5,669.20
1997	6,393.90
1998	6,523.00
1999	7,317.50
2000	7,659.50
2001	8,077.80
2002	9,146.10
2003	9,043.20
2004	9,359.40
2005	8,817.10
2006	9,231.80
2007	9,685.70
2008	9,707.40
2009	10,675.60

Source: Data extracted from **www. the-numbers. com/movies**, February 16, 2010.

FIGURE 2.16

Time-series plot of combined gross of movies per year from 1996 to 2009

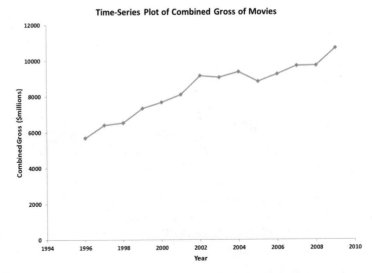

Problems for Section 2.6

LEARNING THE BASICS

2.46 The following is a set of data from a sample of $n = 11$ items:

X:	7	5	8	3	6	0	2	4	9	5	8
Y:	1	5	4	9	8	0	6	2	7	5	4

a. Construct a scatter plot.
b. Is there a relationship between X and Y? Explain.

2.47 The following is a series of annual sales (in millions of dollars) over an 11-year period (2000 to 2010):

Year:	2000	2001	2002	2003	2004	2005	2006	2007	2008	2009	2010
Sales:	13.0	17.0	19.0	20.0	20.5	20.5	20.5	20.0	19.0	17.0	13.0

a. Construct a time-series plot.
b. Does there appear to be any change in annual sales over time? Explain.

APPLYING THE CONCEPTS

✓ SELF Test **2.48** Movie companies need to predict the gross receipts of individual movies once the movie has debuted. The following results, stored in `PotterMovies`, are the first weekend gross, the U.S. gross, and the worldwide gross (in millions of dollars) of the first six Harry Potter movies.

Title	First Weekend	U.S. Gross	Worldwide Gross
Sorcerer's Stone	90.295	317.558	976.458
Chamber of Secrets	88.357	261.988	878.988
Prisoner of Azkaban	93.687	249.539	795.539
Goblet of Fire	102.335	290.013	896.013
Order of the Phoenix	77.108	292.005	938.469
Half-Blood Prince	77.836	301.460	934.601

Source: Data extracted from **www.the-numbers.com/interactive/comp-Harry-Potter.php**.

a. Construct a scatter plot with first weekend gross on the X axis and U.S. gross on the Y axis.
b. Construct a scatter plot with first weekend gross on the X axis and worldwide gross on the Y axis.

c. What can you say about the relationship between first weekend gross and U.S. gross and first weekend gross and worldwide gross?

2.49 The file `VeggieBurger` contains data on the calories and total fat (in grams per serving) for a sample of 12 veggie burgers.

Source: Data extracted from *"Healthful Burgers That Taste Good,"* *Consumer Reports,* June 2008, p 8.

a. Construct a scatter plot with calories on the X axis and total fat on the Y axis.
b. What conclusions can you reach about the relationship between the calories and total fat in veggie burgers?

2.50 College basketball is big business, with coaches' salaries, revenues, and expenses in millions of dollars. The file `College Basketball` contains the coaches' salary and revenue for college basketball at 60 of the 65 schools that played in the 2009 NCAA men's basketball tournament (data extracted from "Compensation for Division 1 Men's Basketball Coaches," *USA Today*, April 2, 2010, p. 8C; and C. Isadore, "Nothing but Net: Basketball Dollars by School," **money.cnn.com/2010/03/18/news/companies/basketball_profits/**).

a. Do you think schools with higher revenues also have higher coaches' salaries?
b. Construct a scatter plot with revenue on the X axis and coaches' salaries on the Y axis.
c. Does the scatter plot confirm or contradict your answer to (a)?

2.51 College football players trying out for the NFL are given the Wonderlic standardized intelligence test. The file `Wonderlic` contains the average Wonderlic scores of football players trying out for the NFL and the graduation rate for football players at selected schools (data extracted from S. Walker, "The NFL's Smartest Team," *The Wall Street Journal*, September 30, 2005, pp. W1, W10).

a. Construct a scatter plot with average Wonderlic score on the X axis and graduation rate on the Y axis.
b. What conclusions can you reach about the relationship between the average Wonderlic score and graduation rate?

2.52 How have stocks performed in the past? The following table presents the data stored in `Stock Performance` that shows the performance of a broad measure of stocks (by percentage) for each decade from the 1830s through the 2000s:

Decade	Performance (%)
1830s	2.8
1840s	12.8
1850s	6.6
1860s	12.5
1870s	7.5
1880s	6.0
1890s	5.5
1900s	10.9
1910s	2.2
1920s	13.3
1930s	−2.2
1940s	9.6
1950s	18.2
1960s	8.3
1970s	6.6
1980s	16.6
1990s	17.6
2000s*	−0.5

* Through December 15, 2009.

Source: Data extracted from T. Lauricella, "Investors Hope the '10s" Beat the '00s," *The Wall Street Journal,* December 21, 2009, pp. C1, C2.

a. Construct a time-series plot of the stock performance from the 1830s to the 2000s.

b. Does there appear to be any pattern in the data?

2.53 According to the U.S. Census Bureau, the average price of a new home declined in 2008 and 2009. The file New Home Prices contains the average price paid for a new

home from 1990 to 2010 (extracted from **www.census.gov,** April 1, 2011).

a. Construct a time-series plot of new home prices.

b. What pattern, if any, is present in the data?

2.54 The following data   (stored in   Movie Attendance) represent the yearly movie attendance (in billions) from 2001 through 2010:

Year	Attendance
2001	1.44
2002	1.60
2003	1.52
2004	1.48
2005	1.38
2006	1.40
2007	1.40
2008	1.36
2009	1.42
2010	1.35

Source: Data extracted from Motion Picture Association of America, **www.mpaa.org**, and S. Bowles, "Ticket Sales Slump at 2010 Box Office," *USA Today,* January 3, 2011, p. 1D.

a. Construct a time-series plot for the movie attendance (in billions).

b. What pattern, if any, is present in the data?

2.55 The file Audits contains the number of audits of corporations with assets of more than $250 million conducted by the Internal Revenue Service (data extracted from K. McCoy, "IRS Audits Big Firms Less Often," *USA Today,* April 15, 2010, p. 1B).

a. Construct a time-series plot.

b. What pattern, if any, is present in the data?

2.7 Organizing Multidimensional Data

In this chapter, you have learned methods for organizing and visualizing a single variable and methods for jointly organizing and visualizing two variables. More and more, businesses need to organize and visualize more than two variables to mine data to discover possible patterns and relationships that simpler explorations might miss. While any number of variables can be used, subject to limits of computation and storage, examples of more than three or four variables can be hard to interpret when simple tables are used to present results. Both Excel and Minitab can organize multidimensional data but the two applications have different strengths: Excel contains **PivotTables**, a type of interactive table that facilitates exploring multidimensional data, while Minitab has specialized statistical and graphing procedures (that are beyond the scope of this book to fully discuss).

Multidimensional Contingency Tables

A **multidimensional contingency table** tallies the responses of three or more categorical variables. In the simplest case of three categorical variables, each cell in the table contains the tallies of the third variable organized by the subgroups represented by the row and column variables.

Consider the Table 2.3 contingency table, which displays the type of fund and whether a fee is charged for the sample of 184 mutual funds. Figure 2.17 presents this table as an Excel PivotTable. Adding a third categorical variable, Risk, to the PivotTable, forms the new multidimensional PivotTable shown in Figure 2.18. The new table reveals that following patterns that cannot be seen in the original Table 2.3 contingency table:

- Although the ratio of fee–yes to fee–no bond funds for the intermediate government category seems to be about 2 to 3 (34 to 53), the ratio for above-average-risk intermediate government bond funds is about 1 to 1 (15 to 14) while the ratio for below average-risk funds is less than 1 to 3 (6 to 20).
- While the group "short-term corporate funds that charge a fee" has nearly equal numbers of above-average-risk, average-risk, and below-average-risk funds (7, 7, and 6), the group "intermediate government bond funds that charge a fee" contains many fewer below-average-risk funds (6) than average risk (13) or above-average (15) ones.
- The pattern of risk tallies differs between the fee–yes and fee–no funds in each of the bond fund categories.

Using methods presented in later chapters, you can confirm whether these first impressions are statistically significant.

FIGURE 2.17

Excel PivotTable version of the Table 2.3 contingency table

	A	B	C	D
1	PivotTable of Type and Fees			
2				
3	Count of Fees	Fees		
4	Type	Yes	No	Grand Total
5	Intermediate Government	34	53	87
6	Short Term Corporate	20	77	97
7	Grand Total	54	130	184

FIGURE 2.18

Excel and Minitab multidimensional contingency table of type, risk, and fees

	A	B	C	D	E
1	Multidimensional Contingency Table of Type, Risk, and Fees				
2					
3	Count of Fees		Fees		
4	Type	Risk	Yes	No	Grand Total
5	Intermediate Government	Above average	15	14	29
6		Average	13	19	32
7		Below average	6	20	26
8	Intermediate Government Total		34	53	87
9	Short Term Corporate	Above average	7	23	30
10		Average	7	30	37
11		Below average	6	24	30
12	Short Term Corporate Total		20	77	97
13	Grand Total		54	130	184

```
Tabulated statistics: Type, Risk, Fees

Rows: Type / Risk   Columns: Fees

                                   No  Yes  All
Intermediate Government
                   Above average   14   15   29
                   Average         19   13   32
                   Below average   20    6   26
Short Term Corporate
                   Above average   23    7   30
                   Average         30    7   37
All                Below average   24    6   30

                   All            130   54  184

Cell Contents:      Count
```

Adding Numerical Variables

Multidimensional contingency tables can contain numerical variables. When you add a numerical variable to a multidimensional analysis, you use categorical variables or variables that represent units of time for the rows and columns that will form the subgroups by which the numerical variable will be analyzed.

For example, Figure 2.19 on page 60 shows a table that cross classifies fees and type in which the cell amounts are the sums of the asset variable for each subgroup, and Figure 2.20 on page 60 shows the same table formatted to show percentages of assets. Comparing Figure 2.21—the table shown in Figure 2.17 but formatted for percentage of the overall total—to Figure 2.20 shows that the percentage of assets for the intermediate government funds by fee category does not mimic the fees category percentages.

FIGURE 2.19

Excel and Minitab multidimensional contingency table of type, fees, and sums of assets

	A	B	C	D
1	Contingency Table of Type, and Fees, and Sums of Assets			
2				
3	Sum of Assets	Fees		
4	Type	Yes	No	Grand Total
5	Intermediate Government	26252.7	56692.2	82944.9
6	Short Term Corporate	16842.1	67772.3	84614.4
7	Grand Total	43094.8	124464.5	167559.3

Tabulated statistics: Type, Fees

```
Rows: Type    Columns: Fees

                              No      Yes      All

Intermediate Government     56692    26253    82945
Short Term Corporate        67772    16842    84614
All                        124465    43095   167559

Cell Contents:  Assets  :  Sum
```

FIGURE 2.20

Multidimensional contingency table of type of fund, fee category, and percentages of assets

	A	B	C	D
1	Contingency Table of Type, and Fees, and Percentages of Assets			
2				
3	Sum of Assets	Fees		
4	Type	Yes	No	Grand Total
5	Intermediate Government	15.67%	33.83%	49.50%
6	Short Term Corporate	10.05%	40.45%	50.50%
7	Grand Total	25.72%	74.28%	100.00%

FIGURE 2.21

Contingency table of type and percentages of fees

	A	B	C	D
1	Contingency Table of Type and Percentages of Fees			
2				
3	Count of Fees	Fees		
4	Type	Yes	No	Grand Total
5	Intermediate Government	18.48%	28.80%	47.28%
6	Short Term Corporate	10.87%	41.85%	52.72%
7	Grand Total	29.35%	70.65%	100.00%

When you include a numerical variable, you typically compute one of the numerical descriptive statistics discussed in Sections 3.1 and 3.2. For example, Figure 2.22 shows a multidimensional contingency table in which the mean, or average 2009 rate of return for each of the subgroups, is computed.[1] This table reveals, among other things, that although there was virtually no difference in the 2009 return depending on whether a fee was charged, for funds with above-average risk, the return was much higher (4.89) for intermediate government funds that charged a fee than for funds that did not charge a fee (1.41).

[1] See Section 3.1 to learn more about the mean.

FIGURE 2.22

Excel and Minitab multidimensional contingency table of type, risk, fees, and the mean 2009 rates of return

	A	B	C	D	E
1	Contingency Table of Type, Risk, Fees and Means of 2009 Return				
2					
3	Average of Return 2009		Fees		
4	Type	Risk	Yes	No	Grand Total
5	Intermediate Government	Above average	4.89	1.41	3.21
6		Average	3.39	3.74	3.60
7		Below average	5.98	7.17	6.90
8	Intermediate Government Total		4.51	4.42	4.45
9	Short Term Corporate	Above average	15.99	12.42	13.25
10		Average	9.87	9.66	9.70
11		Below average	6.53	5.63	5.81
12	Short Term Corporate Total		11.01	9.23	9.60
13	Grand Total		6.92	7.27	7.16

Tabulated statistics: Type, Risk, Fees

```
Rows: Type / Risk   Columns: Fees

                                  No       Yes      All
Intermediate Government
                  Above average  1.407    4.887    3.207
                  Average        3.737    3.392    3.597
                  Below average  7.170    5.983    6.896
Short Term Corporate
                  Above average  12.417  15.986   13.250
                  Average         9.663   9.871    9.703
                  Below average   5.629   6.533    5.810
All
                  All            7.267    6.917    7.164

Cell Contents:  Return 2009  :  Mean
```

Problems for Section 2.7

APPLYING THE CONCEPTS

 2.56 For this problem, use the data in BondFunds2008 .
a. Construct a table that tabulates type, fees, and risk.
b. What conclusions can you reach concerning differences among the types of mutual funds (intermediate government and short-term corporate), based on fees (yes or no) and the risk factor (low, average, and high)?
c. Compare the results of (b) with those shown in Figure 2.18.

2.57 For this problem, use the data in Mutual Funds .
a. Construct a table that tabulates category, objective, and fees.
b. What conclusions can you reach concerning differences among the categories of mutual funds (large cap, medium cap, and small cap), based on objective (growth and value) and fees (yes and no)?

2.58 For this problem, use the data in Mutual Funds .
a. Construct a table that tabulates category, fees, and risk.
b. What conclusions can you reach concerning differences among the categories of mutual funds (large cap, medium cap, and small cap), based on fees (yes and no) and the risk factor (low, average, and high)?

2.59 For this problem, use the data in Mutual Funds .
a. Construct a table that tabulates category, objective, fees, and risk.
b. What conclusions can you reach concerning differences among the categories of mutual funds (large cap, medium cap, and small cap), based on objective (growth and value), the risk factor (low, average, and high), and fees (yes and no)?
c. Which table do you think is easier to interpret, the one in this problem or the ones in Problems 2.56 and 2.57? Explain.

2.8　Misuses and Common Errors in Visualizing Data

Good graphical displays clearly and unambiguously reveal what the data convey. Unfortunately, many graphs presented in the media (broadcast, print, and online) are incorrect, misleading, or so unnecessarily complicated that they should never be used. To illustrate the misuse of graphs, the chart presented in Figure 2.23 is similar to one that was printed in *Time* magazine as part of an article on increasing exports of wine from Australia to the United States.

FIGURE 2.23

"Improper" display of Australian wine exports to the United States, in millions of gallons

Source: *Based on S. Watterson, "Liquid Gold—Australians Are Changing the World of Wine. Even the French Seem Grateful,"* Time, *November 22, 1999, p. 68.*

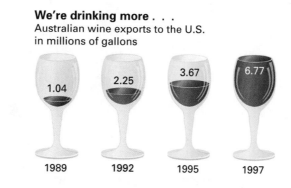

In Figure 2.23, the wineglass icon representing the 6.77 million gallons for 1997 does not appear to be almost twice the size of the wineglass icon representing the 3.67 million gallons for 1995, nor does the wineglass icon representing the 2.25 million gallons for 1992 appear to be twice the size of the wineglass icon representing the 1.04 million gallons for 1989. Part of the reason for this is that the three-dimensional wineglass icon is used to represent the two dimensions of exports and time. Although the wineglass presentation may catch the eye, the data should instead be presented in a summary table or a time-series plot.

In addition to the type of distortion created by the wineglass icons in the *Time* magazine graph displayed in Figure 2.23, improper use of the vertical and horizontal axes leads to distortions. Figure 2.24 presents another graph used in the same *Time* magazine article.

FIGURE 2.24

"Improper" display of amount of land planted with grapes for the wine industry

Source: *Based on S. Watterson, "Liquid Gold—Australians Are Changing the World of Wine. Even the French Seem Grateful," Time, November 22, 1999, pp. 68–69.*

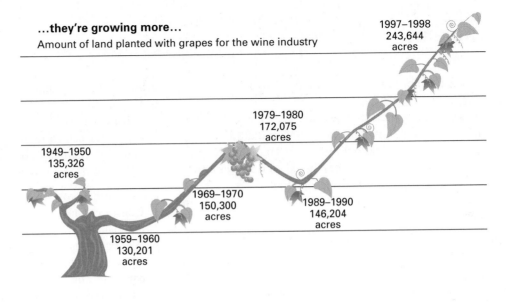

...they're growing more...
Amount of land planted with grapes for the wine industry

1997–1998
243,644
acres

1979–1980
172,075
acres

1949–1950
135,326
acres

1969–1970
150,300
acres

1989–1990
146,204
acres

1959–1960
130,201
acres

There are several problems in this graph. First, there is no zero point on the vertical axis. Second, the acreage of 135,326 for 1949–1950 is plotted above the acreage of 150,300 for 1969–1970. Third, it is not obvious that the difference between 1979–1980 and 1997–1998 (71,569 acres) is approximately 3.5 times the difference between 1979–1980 and 1969–1970 (21,775 acres). Fourth, there are no scale values on the horizontal axis. Years are plotted next to the acreage totals, not on the horizontal axis. Fifth, the values for the time dimension are not properly spaced along the horizontal axis. For example, the value for 1979–1980 is much closer to 1989–1990 than it is to 1969–1970. Other types of eye-catching displays that you typically see in magazines and newspapers often include information that is not necessary and just adds excessive clutter. Figure 2.25 represents one such display.

FIGURE 2.25

"Improper" plot of market share of soft drinks

Source: *Based on Anne B. Carey and Sam Ward, "Coke Still Has Most Fizz," USA Today, May 10, 2000, p. 1B.*

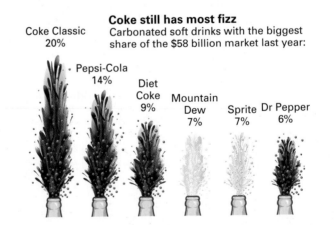

Coke still has most fizz
Carbonated soft drinks with the biggest share of the $58 billion market last year:

Coke Classic
20%

Pepsi-Cola
14%

Diet Coke
9%

Mountain Dew
7%

Sprite
7%

Dr Pepper
6%

The graph in Figure 2.25 shows the products with the largest market share for soft drinks. The graph suffers from too much clutter, although it is designed to show the differences in market share among the soft drinks. The display of the fizz for each soft drink takes up too much of the graph relative to the data. The same information could be better conveyed with a bar chart or pie chart.

The following are some guidelines for developing good graphs:

- A graph should not distort the data.
- A graph should not contain **chartjunk**, unnecessary adornments that convey no useful information.
- Any two-dimensional graph should contain a scale for each axis.
- The scale on the vertical axis should begin at zero.

- All axes should be properly labeled.
- The graph should contain a title.
- The simplest possible graph should be used for a given set of data.

Often individuals unaware of how to construct appropriate graphs violate these guidelines. Some applications, including Excel, tempt you to create "pretty" charts that may be fancy in their designs but that represent unwise choices. For example, making a simple pie chart fancier by adding exploded 3D slices is unwise as this can complicate a viewer's interpretation of the data. Uncommon chart choices such as doughnut, radar, surface, bubble, cone, and pyramid charts may look visually striking, but in most cases they obscure the data.

Problems for Section 2.8

APPLYING THE CONCEPTS

2.60 (Student Project) Bring to class a chart from either a website, newspaper, or magazine published this month that you believe to be a poorly drawn representation of a numerical variable. Be prepared to submit the chart to the instructor with comments about why you believe it is inappropriate. Do you believe that the intent of the chart is to purposely mislead the reader? Also, be prepared to present and comment on this in class.

2.61 (Student Project) Bring to class a chart from either a website, newspaper, or magazine published this month that you believe to be a poorly drawn representation of a categorical variable. Be prepared to submit the chart to the instructor with comments about why you consider it inappropriate. Do you believe that the intent of the chart is to purposely mislead the reader? Also, be prepared to present and comment on this in class.

2.62 (Student Project) The Data and Story Library (DASL) is an online library of data files and stories that illustrate the use of basic statistical methods. Go to **lib.stat.cmu.edu/index.php**, click DASL and explore some of the various graphical displays.
a. Select a graphical display that you think does a good job revealing what the data convey. Discuss why you think it is a good graphical display.
b. Select a graphical display that you think needs a lot of improvement. Discuss why you think that it is a poorly constructed graphical display.

2.63 The following visual display contains an overembellished chart similar to one that appeared in *USA Today*, dealing with the average consumer's Valentine's Day spending ("USA Today Snapshots: The Price of Romance," *USA Today*, February 14, 2007, p. 1B).

Valentine's Day Average Consumer Spending

a. Describe at least one good feature of this visual display.
b. Describe at least one bad feature of this visual display.
c. Redraw the graph, using the guidelines given on page 62 and above.

2.64 The following visual display contains an overembellished chart similar to one that appeared in *USA Today*, dealing with the estimated number of hours the typical American spends using various media ("USA Today Snapshots: Minding Their Media," *USA Today*, March 2, 2007, p. 1B).

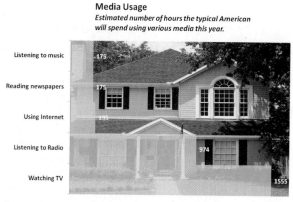

Media Usage
Estimated number of hours the typical American will spend using various media this year.

Courtesy of David Levine

a. Describe at least one good feature of this visual display.

b. Describe at least one bad feature of this visual display.

c. Redraw the graph, using the guidelines given on pages 62–63.

2.65 The following visual display contains an overembellished chart similar to one that appeared in *USA Today*, dealing with which card is safer to use ("USA Today Snapshots: Credit Card vs. Debit Card," *USA Today*, March 14, 2007, p. 1B).

Credit Card vs. Debit Card:
Which one is safer to use?

a. Describe at least one good feature of this visual display.

b. Describe at least one bad feature of this visual display.

c. Redraw the graph, using the guidelines given on pages 62–63.

2.66 Professor Deanna Oxender Burgess of Florida Gulf Coast University conducted research on annual reports of corporations (see D. Rosato, "Worried About the Numbers? How About the Charts?" *The New York Times*, September 15, 2002, p. B7) and found that even slight distortions in a chart changed readers' perception of the information. Using Internet or library sources, select a corporation and study the most recent annual report. Find at least one chart in the report that you think needs improvement and develop an improved version of the chart. Explain why you believe the improved chart is better than the one included in the annual report.

2.67 Figures 2.1 and 2.3 show a bar chart and a pie chart for how adults pay their monthly bills (see pages 40 and 41).

a. Create an exploded pie chart, a doughnut chart, a cone chart, or a pyramid chart that shows how adults pay their monthly bills.

b. Which graphs do you prefer—the bar chart or pie chart or the exploded pie chart, doughnut chart, cone chart, and pyramid chart? Explain.

2.68 Figures 2.2 and 2.4 show a bar chart and a pie chart for the risk level for the bond fund data (see pages 41 and 42).

a. Create an exploded pie chart, a doughnut chart, a cone chart, and a pyramid chart that shows the risk level of bond funds.

b. Which graphs do you prefer—the bar chart or pie chart or the exploded pie chart, doughnut chart, cone chart, and pyramid chart? Explain.

USING STATISTICS @ Choice Is Yours, Part I Revisited

In the Using Statistics scenario, you were hired by the Choice Is Yours investment company to assist clients who seek to invest in mutual funds. A sample of 184 bond mutual funds was selected, and information on the funds and past performance history was recorded. For each of the 184 funds, data were collected on eight variables. With so much information, visualizing all these numbers required the use of properly selected graphical displays.

From bar charts and pie charts, you were able to illustrate that about one-third of the funds were classified as having below-average risk, about one-third had average risk, and about one-third had above-average risk. Cross tabulations of the funds by whether the fund charged a fee and whether the fund invested in intermediate government bonds or short-term corporate bonds revealed that intermediate government bond funds are more likely to charge fees. After constructing histograms on the 2009 return, you were able to conclude that the returns were much higher for the short-term corporate bond funds than for the intermediate government bonds. The return for intermediate government bond funds is concentrated between 0 and 10, whereas the return for the short-term corporate bond funds is concentrated between 5 and 15.

With these insights, you can inform your clients about how the different funds performed. Of course, past performance history does not guarantee future performance. In fact, if you look at returns in 2008, stored in `BondFunds2008`, you will discover that the returns were much *lower* for the short-term corporate bond funds than for the intermediate government bonds!

Using graphical methods such as these is an important first step in summarizing and interpreting data. Although the proper display of data (as discussed in Section 2.8) helps to avoid ambiguity, graphical methods always contain a certain degree of subjectivity. Next, you will need descriptive statistics to further analyze the past performance of the mutual funds. Chapter 3 presents descriptive statistics (e.g., mean, median, and mode).

SUMMARY

Organizing and visualizing data involves using various tables and charts to help draw conclusions about data. In several different chapter examples, tables and charts helped you reach conclusions about how people prefer to pay their bills and about the cost of restaurant meals in a city and its suburbs; they also provided some insights about the sample of bond mutual funds in the Using Statistics scenario.

The tables and charts you use depend on the type of data you have. Table 2.19 summarizes the proper choices for the type of data and the tables and charts discussed in this chapter. In Chapter 3 you will learn about a variety of descriptive statistics useful for data analysis and interpretation.

TABLE 2.19
Selecting Tables and Charts

| Type of Analysis | Type of Data | |
	Numerical	Categorical
Organizing data	Ordered array, frequency distribution, relative frequency distribution, percentage distribution, cumulative percentage distribution (Section 2.3)	Summary table, contingency table (Section 2.2)
Visualizing one variable	Stem-and-leaf display, histogram, percentage polygon, cumulative percentage polygon (ogive) (Section 2.5)	Bar chart, pie chart, Pareto chart (Section 2.4)
Visualizing two variables	Scatter plot, time-series plot (Section 2.6)	Side-by-side bar chart (Section 2.4)
Organizing multidimensional data	Multidimensional tables (Section 2.7)	Multidimensional tables (Section 2.7)

KEY EQUATIONS

Determining the Class Interval Width

$$\text{Interval width} = \frac{\text{highest value} - \text{lowest value}}{\text{number of classes}} \qquad (2.1)$$

Computing the Proportion or Relative Frequency

$$\text{Proportion} = \text{relative frequency} = \frac{\text{number of values in each class}}{\text{total number of values}} \qquad (2.2)$$

KEY TERMS

CHAPTER REVIEW PROBLEMS

CHECKING YOUR UNDERSTANDING

2.69 How do histograms and polygons differ in their construction and use?

2.70 Why would you construct a summary table?

2.71 What are the advantages and disadvantages of using a bar chart, a pie chart, and a Pareto chart?

2.72 Compare and contrast the bar chart for categorical data with the histogram for numerical data.

2.73 What is the difference between a time-series plot and a scatter plot?

2.74 Why is it said that the main feature of a Pareto chart is its ability to separate the "vital few" from the "trivial many"?

2.75 What are the three different ways to break down the percentages in a contingency table?

2.76 How can a multidimensional table differ from a two variable contingency table?

2.77 What type of insights can you gain from a three-way table that are not available in a two-way table?

APPLYING THE CONCEPTS

2.78 The following summary table presents the breakdown of the price of a new college textbook:

Revenue Category	Percentage (%)	
Publisher	64.8	
Manufacturing costs		32.3
Marketing and promotion		15.4
Administrative costs and taxes		10.0
After-tax profit		7.1
Bookstore	22.4	
Employee salaries and benefits		11.3
Operations		6.6
Pretax profit		4.5
Author	11.6	
Freight	1.2	

Source: Data extracted from T. Lewin, "When Books Break the Bank," *The New York Times,* September 16, 2003, pp. B1, B4.

a. Using the four categories publisher, bookstore, author, and freight, construct a bar chart, a pie chart, and a Pareto chart.
b. Using the four subcategories of publisher and three subcategories of bookstore, along with the author and freight categories, construct a Pareto chart.
c. Based on the results of (a) and (b), what conclusions can you reach concerning who gets the revenue from the

sales of new college textbooks? Do any of these results surprise you? Explain.

2.79 The following table represents the market share (in number of movies, gross in millions of dollars, and in number of tickets sold in millions) of each type of movie in 2009:

Type	Number	Gross ($ millions)	Tickets (millions)
Based on book/short story	66	2042.9	272.4
Based on comic/graphic novel	6	376.2	50.2
Based on factual book/article	5	280.7	37.4
Based on game	3	9.2	1.2
Based on musical/opera	1	13.7	1.8
Based on play	8	172.0	22.9
Based on real life events	95	334.9	44.7
Based on toy	1	150.2	20.0
Based on TV	7	267.5	35.7
Compilation	1	0.6	0.1
Original screenplay	203	4,335.7	578.1
Remake	18	422.6	56.3
Sequel	20	2,064.2	275.2
Spin-off	1	179.9	24.0

Source: Data extracted from **www.the-numbers.com/market/Sources2009.php**.

a. Construct a bar chart, a pie chart, and a Pareto chart for the number of movies, gross (in millions of dollars), and number of tickets sold (in millions).
b. What conclusions can you reach about the market share of the different types of movies in 2009?

2.80 A survey was conducted from 665 consumer magazines on the practices of their websites. The results are summarized in a copyediting table and a fact-checking table:

Copyediting as Compared to Print Content	Percentage
As rigorous	41
Less rigorous	48
Not copyedited	11

a. For copyediting, construct a bar chart, a pie chart, and a Pareto chart.
b. Which graphical method do you think is best for portraying these data?

Fact Checking as Compared to Print Content	Percentage
Same	57
Less rigorous	27
Online not fact checked	8
Neither online nor print is fact-checked	8

Source: Data extracted from S. Clifford, "Columbia Survey Finds a Slack Editing Process of Magazine Web Sites," *The New York Times*, March 1, 2010, p. B6.

c. For fact checking, construct a bar chart, a pie chart, and a Pareto chart.
d. Which graphical method do you think is best for portraying these data?
e. What conclusions can you reach concerning copy editing and fact checking of print and online consumer magazines?

2.81 The owner of a restaurant that serves Continental-style entrées has the business objective of learning more about the patterns of patron demand during the Friday-to-Sunday weekend time period. Data were collected from 630 customers on the type of entrée ordered and organized in the following table:

Type of Entrée	Number Served
Beef	187
Chicken	103
Mixed	30
Duck	25
Fish	122
Pasta	63
Shellfish	74
Veal	26
Total	630

a. Construct a percentage summary table for the types of entrées ordered.
b. Construct a bar chart, a pie chart, and a Pareto chart for the types of entrées ordered.
c. Do you prefer using a Pareto chart or a pie chart for these data? Why?
d. What conclusions can the restaurant owner reach concerning demand for different types of entrées?

2.82 Suppose that the owner of the restaurant in Problem 2.81 also wanted to study the demand for dessert during the same time period. She decided that in addition to studying whether a dessert was ordered, she would also study the gender of the individual and whether a beef entrée was ordered. Data were collected from 600 customers and organized in the following contingency tables:

DESSERT ORDERED	GENDER		
	Male	Female	Total
Yes	40	96	136
No	240	224	464
Total	280	320	600

DESSERT ORDERED	BEEF ENTRÉE		
	Yes	No	Total
Yes	71	65	136
No	116	348	464
Total	187	413	600

a. For each of the two contingency tables, construct contingency tables of row percentages, column percentages, and total percentages.
b. Which type of percentage (row, column, or total) do you think is most informative for each gender? For beef entrée? Explain.
c. What conclusions concerning the pattern of dessert ordering can the restaurant owner reach?

2.83 The following data represent the pounds per capita of fresh food and packaged food consumed in the United States, Japan, and Russia in 2009:

FRESH FOOD	COUNTRY		
	United States	Japan	Russia
Eggs, nuts, and beans	88	94	88
Fruit	124	126	88
Meat and seafood	197	146	125
Vegetables	194	278	335

a. For the United States, Japan, and Russia, construct a bar chart, a pie chart, and a Pareto chart for different types of fresh foods consumed.

PACKAGED FOOD	COUNTRY		
	United States	Japan	Russia
Bakery goods	108	53	144
Dairy products	298	147	127
Pasta	12	32	16
Processed, frozen, dried and chilled food, and ready-to-eat meals	183	251	70
Sauces, dressings, and condiments	63	75	49
Snacks and candy	47	19	24
Soup and canned food	77	17	25

Source: Data extracted from H. Fairfield, "Factory Food," *The New York Times,* April 4, 2010, p. BU5.

b. For the United States, Japan, and Russia, construct a bar chart, a pie chart, and a Pareto chart for different types of packaged foods consumed.
c. What conclusions can you reach concerning differences between the United States, Japan, and Russia in the fresh foods and packaged foods consumed?

2.84 In 2000, a growing number of warranty claims on Firestone tires sold on Ford SUVs prompted Firestone and Ford to issue a major recall. An analysis of warranty claims data helped identify which models to recall. A breakdown of 2,504 warranty claims based on tire size is given in the following table:

Tire Size	Number of Warranty Claims
23575R15	2,030
311050R15	137
30950R15	82
23570R16	81
331250R15	58
25570R16	54
Others	62

Source: Data extracted from Robert L. Simison, "Ford Steps Up Recall Without Firestone," *The Wall Street Journal,* August 14, 2000, p. A3.

The 2,030 warranty claims for the 23575R15 tires can be categorized into ATX models and Wilderness models. The type of incident leading to a warranty claim, by model type, is summarized in the following table:

Incident Type	ATX Model Warranty Claims	Wilderness Warranty Claims
Tread		
separation	1,365	59
Blowout	77	41
Other/		
unknown	422	66
Total	1,864	166

Source: Data extracted from Robert L. Simison, "Ford Steps Up Recall Without Firestone," *The Wall Street Journal,* August 14, 2000, p. A3.

a. Construct a Pareto chart for the number of warranty claims by tire size. What tire size accounts for most of the claims?

b. Construct a pie chart to display the percentage of the total number of warranty claims for the 23575R15 tires that come from the ATX model and Wilderness model. Interpret the chart.

c. Construct a Pareto chart for the type of incident causing the warranty claim for the ATX model. Does a certain type of incident account for most of the claims?

d. Construct a Pareto chart for the type of incident causing the warranty claim for the Wilderness model. Does a certain type of incident account for most of the claims?

2.85 One of the major measures of the quality of service provided by an organization is the speed with which the organization responds to customer complaints. A large family-held department store selling furniture and flooring, including carpet, had undergone a major expansion in the past several years. In particular, the flooring department had expanded from 2 installation crews to an installation supervisor, a measurer, and 15 installation crews. A business objective of the company was to reduce the time between when the complaint is received and when it is resolved. During a recent year, the company received 50 complaints concerning carpet installation. The data from the 50 complaints, stored in Furniture , represent the number of days between the receipt of the complaint and the resolution of the complaint:

54	5	35	137	31	27	152	2	123	81	74	27
11	19	126	110	110	29	61	35	94	31	26	5
12	4	165	32	29	28	29	26	25	1	14	13
13	10	5	27	4	52	30	22	36	26	20	23
33	68										

a. Construct a frequency distribution and a percentage distribution.

b. Construct a histogram and a percentage polygon.

c. Construct a cumulative percentage distribution and plot a cumulative percentage polygon (ogive).

d. On the basis of the results of (a) through (c), if you had to tell the president of the company how long a customer should expect to wait to have a complaint resolved, what would you say? Explain.

2.86 The file DomesticBeer contains the percentage alcohol, number of calories per 12 ounces, and number of carbohydrates (in grams) per 12 ounces for 145 of the best-selling domestic beers in the United States.

Source: Data extracted from **www.Beer100.com,** April 1, 2011.

a. Construct a percentage histogram for each of the three variables.

b. Construct three scatter plots: percentage alcohol versus calories, percentage alcohol versus carbohydrates, and calories versus carbohydrates.

c. Discuss what you learn from studying the graphs in (a) and (b).

2.87 The file CigaretteTax contains the state cigarette tax ($) for each state as of December 31, 2010.

a. Construct an ordered array.

b. Plot a percentage histogram.

c. What conclusions can you reach about the differences in the state cigarette tax between the states?

2.88 The file CDRate contains the yields for a one-year certificate of deposit (CD) and a five-year certificate of deposit (CD) for 25 banks in the United States, as of April 4, 2011.

Source: Data extracted from **www.Bankrate.com,** April 4, 2011.

a. Construct a stem-and-leaf display for each variable.

b. Construct a scatter plot of one-year CD versus five-year CD.

c. What is the relationship between the one-year CD rate and the five-year CD rate?

2.89 The file CEO-Compensation includes the total compensation (in millions of $) of CEOs of 161 large public companies and the investment return in 2010. For total compensation:

Source: Data extracted from M. Krantz and B. Hansen, "CEO Pay Sours While Workers' Pay Stalls," "Bargains in the Boardroom," *USA Today,* April 1, 2011, pp. 1B, 2B, and **money.usatoday.com**

a. Construct a frequency distribution and a percentage distribution.

b. Construct a histogram and a percentage polygon.

c. Construct a cumulative percentage distribution and plot a cumulative percentage polygon (ogive).

d. Based on (a) through (c), what conclusions can you reach concerning CEO compensation in 2010?

e. Construct a scatter plot of total compensation and investment return in 2010.

f. What is the relationship between the total compensation and investment return in 2010?

2.90 Studies conducted by a manufacturer of Boston and Vermont asphalt shingles have shown product weight to be a major factor in customers' perception of quality. Moreover, the weight represents the amount of raw materials being used and is therefore very important to the company from a cost standpoint. The last stage of the assembly line packages the shingles before the packages are placed on wooden pallets. The variable of interest is the weight in pounds of the pallet which for most brands holds 16 squares of shingles. The company expects pallets of its Boston brand-name shingles to weigh at least 3,050 pounds but less than 3,260 pounds. For the company's Vermont brand-name shingles, pallets should weigh at least 3,600 pounds but less than 3,800. Data are collected from a sample of 368 pallets of Boston shingles and 330 pallets of Vermont shingles and stored in Pallet .

a. For the Boston shingles, construct a frequency distribution and a percentage distribution having eight class intervals, using 3,015, 3,050, 3,085, 3,120, 3,155, 3,190, 3,225, 3,260, and 3,295 as the class boundaries.

b. For the Vermont shingles, construct a frequency distribution and a percentage distribution having seven class intervals, using 3,550, 3,600, 3,650, 3,700, 3,750, 3,800, 3,850, and 3,900 as the class boundaries.

c. Construct percentage histograms for the Boston shingles and for the Vermont shingles.

d. Comment on the distribution of pallet weights for the Boston and Vermont shingles. Be sure to identify the percentage of pallets that are underweight and overweight.

2.91 What was the average price of a room at two-star, three-star, and four-star hotels in cities around the world in the summer of 2010? The file HotelPrices contains the prices in English pounds (about US $1.56 as of January 2011). Complete the following for two-star, three-star, and four-star hotels.
Source: Data extracted from **http://www.hotels.com/press/hotel-price-index-summer-2010.html.**

a. Construct a frequency distribution and a percentage distribution.

b. Construct a histogram and a percentage polygon.

c. Construct a cumulative percentage distribution and plot a cumulative percentage polygon (ogive).

d. What conclusions can you reach about the cost of two-star, three-star, and four-star hotels?

e. Construct separate scatter plots of the cost of two-star hotels versus three-star hotels, two-star hotels versus four-star hotels, and three-star hotels versus four-star hotels.

f. What conclusions can you reach about the relationship of the price of two-star, three-star, and four-star hotels?

2.92 The file Protein contains calorie and cholesterol information for popular protein foods (fresh red meats, poultry, and fish).
Source: U.S. Department of Agriculture.

a. Construct a percentage histogram for the number of calories.

b. Construct a percentage histogram for the amount of cholesterol.

c. What conclusions can you reach from your analyses in (a) and (b)?

2.93 The file Natural Gas contains the monthly average wellhead and residential price for natural gas (dollars per thousand cu. ft.) in the United States from January 1, 2008, to January 1, 2011. For the wellhead price and the residential price:
Source: "Energy Information Administration," **www.eia.doe.gov**, April 4, 2011.

a. Construct a time-series plot.

b. What pattern, if any, is present in the data?

c. Construct a scatter plot of the wellhead price and the residential price.

d. What conclusion can you reach about the relationship between the wellhead price and the residential price?

2.94 The following data (stored in Drink) represent the amount of soft drink in a sample of 50 consecutively filled 2-liter bottles. The results are listed horizontally in the order of being filled:

2.109 2.086 2.066 2.075 2.065 2.057 2.052 2.044 2.036 2.038
2.031 2.029 2.025 2.029 2.023 2.020 2.015 2.014 2.013 2.014
2.012 2.012 2.012 2.010 2.005 2.003 1.999 1.996 1.997 1.992
1.994 1.986 1.984 1.981 1.973 1.975 1.971 1.969 1.966 1.967
1.963 1.957 1.951 1.951 1.947 1.941 1.941 1.938 1.908 1.894

a. Construct a time-series plot for the amount of soft drink on the Y axis and the bottle number (going consecutively from 1 to 50) on the X axis.

b. What pattern, if any, is present in these data?

c. If you had to make a prediction about the amount of soft drink filled in the next bottle, what would you predict?

d. Based on the results of (a) through (c), explain why it is important to construct a time-series plot and not just a histogram, as was done in Problem 2.45 on page 54.

2.95 The file Currency contains the exchange rates of the Canadian dollar, the Japanese yen, and the English pound from 1980 to 2010 where the Canadian dollar, the Japanese yen, and the English pound are expressed in units per U.S. dollar.

a. Construct time-series plots for the yearly closing values of the Canadian dollar, the Japanese yen, and the English pound.

b. Explain any patterns present in the plots.

c. Write a short summary of your findings.

d. Construct separate scatter plots of the value of the Canadian dollar versus the Japanese yen, the Canadian dollar versus the English pound, and the Japanese yen versus the English pound.

e. What conclusions can you reach concerning the value of the Canadian dollar, Japanese yen, and English pound in terms of the U.S. dollar?

2.96 (Class Project) Have each student in the class respond to the question "Which carbonated soft drink do you most prefer?" so that the instructor can tally the results into a summary table.

a. Convert the data to percentages and construct a Pareto chart.

b. Analyze the findings.

2.97 (Class Project) Let each student in the class be cross-classified on the basis of gender (male, female) and current employment status (yes, no) so that the instructor can tally the results.

a. Construct a table with either row or column percentages, depending on which you think is more informative.

b. What would you conclude from this study?

c. What other variables would you want to know regarding employment in order to enhance your findings?

REPORT WRITING EXERCISES

2.98 Referring to the results from Problem 2.90 on page 70 concerning the weight of Boston and Vermont shingles, write a report that evaluates whether the weight of the pallets of the two types of shingles are what the company expects. Be sure to incorporate tables and charts into the report.

2.99 Referring to the results from Problem 2.84 on pages 68–69 concerning the warranty claims on Firestone tires, write a report that evaluates warranty claims on Firestone tires sold on Ford SUVs. Be sure to incorporate tables and charts into the report.

TEAM PROJECT

The file **Bond Funds** contains information regarding nine variables from a sample of 184 mutual funds:

Fund number—Identification number for each bond fund
Type—Bond fund type (intermediate government or short-term corporate)
Assets—In millions of dollars
Fees—Sales charges (no or yes)
Expense ratio—Ratio of expenses to net assets in percentage
Return 2009—Twelve-month return in 2009
Three-year return—Annualized return, 2007–2009
Five-year return—Annualized return, 2005–2009
Risk—Risk-of-loss factor of the mutual fund (below average, average, or above average)

2.100 For this problem, consider the expense ratio.

a. Construct a percentage histogram.

b. Using a single graph, plot percentage polygons of the expense ratio for bond funds that have fees and bond funds that do not have fees.

c. What conclusions about the expense ratio can you reach, based on the results of (a) and (b)?

2.101 For this problem, consider the three-year annualized return from 2007 to 2009.

a. Construct a percentage histogram.

b. Using a single graph, plot percentage polygons of the three-year annualized return from 2007 to 2009 for intermediate government funds and short-term corporate funds.

c. What conclusions about the three-year annualized return from 2007 to 2009 can you reach, based on the results of (a) and (b)?

2.102 For this problem, consider the five-year annualized return from 2005 to 2009.

a. Construct a percentage histogram.

b. Using a single graph, plot percentage polygons of the five-year annualized return from 2005 to 2009 for intermediate government funds and short-term corporate funds.

c. What conclusions about the five-year annualized return from 2005 to 2009 can you reach, based on the results of (a) and (b)?

STUDENT SURVEY DATABASE

2.103 Problem 1.27 on the page 13 describes a survey of 62 undergraduate students (stored in **UndergradSurvey**). For these data, construct all the appropriate tables and charts and write a report summarizing your conclusions.

2.104 Problem 2.103 describes a survey of 62 undergraduate students (stored in **UndergradSurvey**).

a. Select a sample of undergraduate students at your school and conduct a similar survey for those students.

b. For the data collected in (a), construct all the appropriate tables and charts and write a report summarizing your conclusions.

c. Compare the results of (b) to those of Problem 2.103.

2.105 Problem 1.28 on the page 14 describes a survey of 44 graduate students (see the file **GradSurvey**). For these data, construct all appropriate tables and charts and write a report summarizing your conclusions.

2.106 Problem 2.105 describes a survey of 44 MBA students (stored in **GradSurvey**).

a. Select a sample of MBA students in your MBA program and conduct a similar survey for those students.

b. For the data collected in (a), construct all the appropriate tables and charts and write a report summarizing your conclusions.

c. Compare the results of (b) to those of Problem 2.105.

MANAGING ASHLAND MULTICOMM SERVICES

Recently, Ashland MultiComm Services has been criticized for its inadequate customer service in responding to questions and problems about its telephone, cable television, and Internet services. Senior management has established a task force charged with the business objective of improving customer service. In response to this charge, the task force collected data about the types of customer service errors, the cost of customer service errors, and the cost of wrong billing errors. It found the following data:

Types of Customer Service Errors

Type of Errors	Frequency
Incorrect accessory	27
Incorrect address	42
Incorrect contact phone	31
Invalid wiring	9
On-demand programming error	14
Subscription not ordered	8
Suspension error	15
Termination error	22
Website access error	30
Wrong billing	137
Wrong end date	17
Wrong number of connections	19
Wrong price quoted	20
Wrong start date	24
Wrong subscription type	33
Total	448

Cost of Customer Service Errors in the Past Year

Type of Errors	Cost ($ thousands)
Incorrect accessory	17.3
Incorrect address	62.4
Incorrect contact phone	21.3
Invalid wiring	40.8
On-demand programming errors	38.8
Subscription not ordered	20.3
Suspension error	46.8
Termination error	50.9
Website access errors	60.7
Wrong billing	121.7
Wrong end date	40.9
Wrong number of connections	28.1
Wrong price quoted	50.3
Wrong start date	40.8
Wrong subscription type	60.1
Total	701.2

Type and Cost of Wrong Billing Errors

Type of Wrong Billing Errors	Cost ($ thousands)
Declined or held transactions	7.6
Incorrect account number	104.3
Invalid verification	9.8
Total	121.7

1. Review these data (stored in AMS2-1). Identify the variables that are important in describing the customer service problems. For each variable you identify, construct the graphical representation you think is most appropriate and explain your choice. Also, suggest what other information concerning the different types of errors would be useful to examine. Offer possible courses of action for either the task force or management to take that would support the goal of improving customer service.

2. As a follow-up activity, the task force decides to collect data to study the pattern of calls to the help desk (stored in AMS2-2). Analyze these data and present your conclusions in a report.

DIGITAL CASE

In the Using Statistics scenario, you were asked to gather information to help make wise investment choices. Sources for such information include brokerage firms, investment counselors, and other financial services firms. Apply your knowledge about the proper use of tables and charts in this Digital Case about the claims of foresight and excellence by an Ashland-area financial services firm.

Open **EndRunGuide.pdf,** which contains the EndRun Financial Services "Guide to Investing." Review the guide, paying close attention to the company's investment claims and supporting data and then answer the following.

1. How does the presentation of the general information about EndRun in this guide affect your perception of the business?

2. Is EndRun's claim about having more winners than losers a fair and accurate reflection of the quality of its investment service? If you do not think that the claim is a fair and accurate one, provide an alternate presentation that you think is fair and accurate.

3. Review the discussion about EndRun's "Big Eight Difference" and then open and examine Mutual Funds, a sample of mutual funds. Are there any other relevant data from that file that could have been included in the Big Eight table? How would the new data alter your perception of EndRun's claims?

4. EndRun is proud that all Big Eight funds have gained in value over the past five years. Do you agree that EndRun should be proud of its selections? Why or why not?

REFERENCES

1. Huff, D., *How to Lie with Statistics* (New York: Norton, 1954).
2. Levine, D. and D. Stephan, "Teaching Introductory Business Statistics Using the DCOVA Framework," *Decision Sciences Journal of Innovative Education*, 9, September 2011, p. 393–398.
3. *Microsoft Excel 2010* (Redmond, WA: Microsoft Corporation, 2010).
4. *Minitab Release 16* (State College, PA: Minitab, Inc., 2010).
5. Tufte, E. R., *Beautiful Evidence* (Cheshire, CT: Graphics Press, 2006).
6. Tufte, E. R., *Envisioning Information* (Cheshire, CT: Graphics Press, 1990).
7. Tufte, E. R., *The Visual Display of Quantitative Information*, 2nd ed. (Cheshire, CT: Graphics Press, 2002).
8. Tufte, E. R., *Visual Explanations* (Cheshire, CT: Graphics Press, 1997).
9. Wainer, H., *Visual Revelations: Graphical Tales of Fate and Deception from Napoleon Bonaparte to Ross Perot* (New York: Copernicus/Springer-Verlag, 1997).

CHAPTER 2 EXCEL GUIDE

EG2.2 ORGANIZING CATEGORICAL DATA

The Summary Table

PHStat2 Use **One-Way Tables & Charts** to create a summary table. For example, to create a summary table similar to Table 2.2 on page 28, open to the **DATA worksheet** of the **Bond Funds workbook**. Select **PHStat → Descriptive Statistics → One-Way Tables & Charts**. In the procedure's dialog box (shown below):

1. Click **Raw Categorical Data**.
2. Enter **I1:I185** as the **Raw Data Cell Range** and check **First cell contains label**.
3. Enter a **Title**, check **Percentage Column**, and click **OK**.

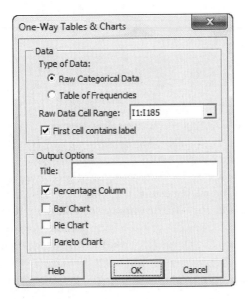

The DATA worksheet contains unsummarized data. For data that have already been tallied into categories, click **Table of Frequencies**.

In-Depth Excel For data that need to be tallied, use the PivotTable feature to create a summary table. (For the case in which data have already been tallied, use the **SUMMARY_SIMPLE worksheet** of the **Chapter 2 workbook** as a model for creating a summary table.)

For example, to create a summary table similar to Table 2.2 on page 28, open to the **DATA worksheet** of the **Bond Funds workbook** and select **Insert → PivotTable**. In the Create PivotTable dialog box (shown at the top of the next column):

1. Click **Select a table or range** and enter **I1:I185** as the **Table/Range** cell range.
2. Click **New Worksheet** and then click **OK**.

In the PivotTable Field List task pane (shown below):

3. Check **Risk** in the **Choose fields to add to report** box.
4. Drag the checked **Risk** label and drop it in the **Row Labels** box. Drag a second copy of this checked **Risk** label and drop it in the **Σ Values** box. This second label changes to **Count of Risk** to indicate that a count, or tally, of the occurrences of each risk category will be displayed in the PivotTable.

In the PivotTable being created:

5. Right-click and then click **PivotTable Options** in the shortcut menu that appears.

In the PivotTable Options dialog box (shown below):

6. Click the **Layout & Format** tab.

7. Check **For empty cells show** and enter **0** as its value. Leave all other settings unchanged.

8. Click **OK** to complete the PivotTable.

To add a column for the percentage frequency:

9. Enter **Percentage** in cell C4. Enter the formula **=B5/B$8** in cell **C5** and copy it down through row 7.

10. Select cell range **C5:E5**, right-click, and select **Format Cells** in the shortcut menu.

11. In the **Number** tab of the Format Cells dialog box, select **Percentage** as the **Category** and click **OK**.

12. Adjust cell borders, if desired (see Appendix F).

The Contingency Table

PHStat2 Use **Two-Way Tables & Charts** to create a contingency table for data that need to be tallied. For example, to create the Table 2.3 contingency table on page 29, open to the **DATA worksheet** of the **Bond Funds workbook**. Select **PHStat → Descriptive Statistics →**

Two-Way Tables & Charts. In the procedure's dialog box (shown below):

1. Enter **B1:B185** as the **Row Variable Cell Range**.

2. Enter **D1:D185** as the **Column Variable Cell Range**.

3. Check **First cell in each range contains label**.

4. Enter a **Title** and click **OK**.

After the procedure creates the PivotTable, rearrange the order of the "No" and "Yes" columns:

5. Click the **Fees** drop-down list in cell B3 and select **Sort Z to A**.

In-Depth Excel For data that need to be tallied, use the PivotTable feature to create a contingency table. (For the case in which data have already been tallied, use the **CONTINGENCY_SIMPLE worksheet** of the **Chapter 2 workbook** as a model for creating a contingency table.) For example, to create the Table 2.3 contingency table on page 29, open to the **DATA worksheet** of the **Bond Funds workbook**. Select **Insert → PivotTable**. In the Create PivotTable dialog box:

1. Click **Select a table or range** and enter **B1:D185** as the **Table/Range** cell range. (Although **Type** is in column B and **Fees** is in column D, Excel does not allow you to enter a range comprised of nonadjacent columns.)

2. Click **New Worksheet** and then click **OK**.

In the PivotTable Field List task pane (shown at the top of page 76):

3. Check **Type** and **Fees** in the **Choose fields to add to report** box.

4. Drag the checked **Type** label and drop it in the **Row Labels** box.

5. Drag a second copy of the check **Type** label and drop it in the Σ **Values** box. (This label changes to **Count of Type**.) Then drag the checked **Fees** label and drop it in the **Column Labels** area.

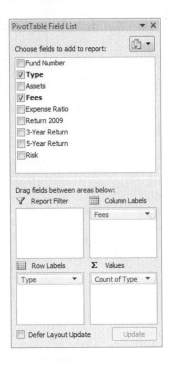

In the PivotTable being created:

6. Click the **Fees** drop-down list in cell B3 and select **Sort Z to A** to rearrange the order of the "No" and "Yes" columns.

7. Right-click and then click **PivotTable Options** in the shortcut menu that appears.

In the PivotTable Options dialog box:

8. Click the **Layout & Format** tab.

9. Check **For empty cells show** and enter **0** as its value. Leave all other settings unchanged.

10. Click the **Total & Filters** tab.

11. Check **Show grand totals for columns** and **Show grand totals for rows**.

12. Click **OK** to complete the table.

EG2.3 ORGANIZING NUMERICAL DATA

Stacked and Unstacked Data

PHStat2 Use **Stack Data** or **Unstack Data** to rearrange data. For example, to unstack the **Return 2009** variable in column F of the **DATA worksheet** of the **Bond Funds workbook**, open to that worksheet. Select **Data Preparation → Unstack Data**. In that procedure's dialog box, enter **B1:B185** (the Type variable cell range) as the **Grouping Variable Cell Range** and enter **F1:F185** as the **Stacked Data Cell Range**. Check **First cells in both ranges contain label** and click **OK**. The unstacked data appears on a new worksheet.

The Ordered Array

In-Depth Excel To create an ordered array, first select the data to be sorted. Then select **Home → Sort & Filter** (in the **Editing group**) → **Sort Smallest to Largest**.

The Frequency Distribution, Part I

To create a frequency distribution, you must first translate your classes into what Excel calls *bins*. Bins approximate the classes of a frequency distribution. Unlike classes, bins do not have precise lower and upper boundary values. You establish bins by entering, in ascending order, a list of "bin numbers" into a column cell range. Each bin number, in turn, defines a bin: A bin is all the values that are less than or equal to its bin number and that are greater than the previous bin number.

Because the first bin number does not have a "previous" bin number, the first bin can never have a precise lower boundary value, as a first class always has. A common workaround to this problem, used in the examples throughout this book, is to define an extra bin, using a bin number that is slightly lower than the lower boundary value of the first class. This extra bin number, appearing first, will allow the now-second bin number to better approximate the first class, though at the cost of adding an unwanted bin to the results.

In this chapter, Tables 2.8 through 2.11 on pages 34–36 use class groupings in the form "*valueA* but less than *valueB*." You can translate class groupings in this form into nearly equivalent bins by creating a list of bin numbers that are slightly lower than each *valueB* that appears in the class groupings. For example, the Table 2.9 classes on page 34 could be translated into nearly equivalent bins by using this bin number list: −10.01 (the extra bin number), −5.01 ("slightly less" than −5), −0.01, 4.99 (slightly less than 5), 9.99, 14.99, 19.99, 24.99, 29.99, and 34.99.

For class groupings in the form "all values from *valueA* to *valueB*," such as the set 0.0 through 4.9, 5.0 through 9.9, 10.0 through 14.9, and 15.0 through 19.9, you can approximate each class grouping by choosing a bin number slightly more than each *valueB*, as in this list of bin numbers: −0.01 (the extra bin number), 4.99 (slightly more than 4.9), 9.99, 14.99, and 19.99.

Use an empty column in the worksheet that contains your untallied data to enter your bin numbers (in ascending order). Enter **Bins** in the row 1 cell of that column as the column heading. Enter your bin numbers before you use the Part II instructions to create frequency distributions.

When you create your own frequency distributions, you can include frequency, percentage, and/or cumulative percentages as columns of one distribution, unlike what is shown in Tables 2.8 through 2.11. Also, when you use Excel, you create frequency distributions for individual categories separately (e.g., a frequency distribution for intermediate government bond funds, followed by one for short-term corporate bond funds). To form worksheets that look like two-category Tables 2.8 through 2.11, you cut and paste parts of separately created frequency distributions. (Examine the **FD_IG** and **FD_STC** worksheets of the **Chapter 2 workbook** and then examine the **FD_COMBINED worksheet** to see how frequency distributions for an individual category can be cut and pasted to form one table.)

The Frequency Distribution, Part II

PHStat2 Use **Frequency Distribution** to create a frequency distribution. For example, to create the Table 2.9 frequency distribution on page 34, open to the **DATA worksheet** of the **Bond Funds workbook**. Select **PHStat → Descriptive Statistics → Frequency Distribution**. In the procedure's dialog box (shown below):

1. Enter **F1:F185** as the **Variable Cell Range**, enter **J1:J11** as the **Bins Cell Range**, and check **First cell in each range contains label**.

2. Click **Multiple Groups - Stacked** and enter **B1:B185** as the **Grouping Variable Cell Range**. (In the DATA worksheet, the 2009 returns for both types of bond funds are stacked, or placed in a single column. The column B values allow PHStat2 to unstack the returns for intermediate government funds from the returns for the short-term corporate funds.)

3. Enter a **Title** and click **OK**.

When creating other frequency distributions, if you use a worksheet that contains data for a single group, such as the **IGDATA** or **STCDATA worksheets**, click **Single Group Variable** in step 2. Note that the **Histogram & Polygons** procedure, discussed in Section EG2.5, also creates frequency distributions.

In-Depth Excel Use the **FREQUENCY** worksheet function and a bin number list (see "The Frequency Distribution, Part I" on page 76) to create a frequency distribution.

For example, to create the Table 2.9 frequency distribution on page 34, open to and review the **IGDATA** and **STCDATA worksheets** of the **Bond Funds workbook**. Note that the worksheets divide the bond funds sample by fund type and that the two worksheets contain identical bin number lists in column J. With the workbook open to the IGDATA worksheet:

1. Right-click the **IGDATA sheet tab** and then click **Insert** in the shortcut menu. In the Insert dialog box, click the **Worksheet** icon and click **OK** to insert a new worksheet.

2. In the new worksheet, enter a worksheet title in cell **A1**, **Bins** in cell **A3**, and **Frequency** in cell **B3**.

3. Copy the **bin number list** that is in the cell range **J2:J11** of the IGDATA worksheet and paste this list into column A of the new worksheet, starting with cell **A4**.

4. Select the cell range **B4:B13** that will contain the frequency function.

5. Type, but do not press the **Enter** or **Tab** key, the formula **=FREQUENCY(IGDATA!$F$1:$F$88, $A$4:$A$13)**. Then, while holding down the **Ctrl** and **Shift** keys (or the **Apple** key on a Mac), press the **Enter** key. (This combination keystroke enters an "array formula," explained in Appendix F, in the cell range **B4:B13**.)

To create the frequency distribution for short-term corporate bonds, repeat steps 1 through 5 but enter the formula **=FREQUENCY(STCDATA!$F$1:$F$98, $A$4:$A$13)** in step 5. Then cut and paste the results from the two frequency distributions to create a table similar to Table 2.9.

Note that in step 5, you entered the cell range as **IGDATA!$F$1:$F$88** (or **STCDATA!$F$1:$F$98**) and not as **F1:F88** (or **F1:F98**) because the data to be summarized are located on another worksheet, and you wanted to use absolute cell references to facilitate the copying of the frequency column to create a table similar to Table 2.9.

Analysis ToolPak Use **Histogram** with a bin number list (see "The Frequency Distribution, Part I" on page 76) to create a frequency distribution. For example, to create the Table 2.9 frequency distribution on page 34, open to the **IGDATA worksheet** of the **Bond Funds workbook** and select **Data → Data Analysis**. In the Data Analysis dialog box, select **Histogram** from the **Analysis Tools** list and then click **OK**. In the Histogram dialog box (see the top of page 78):

1. Enter **F1:F88** as the **Input Range** and enter **J1:J11** as the **Bin Range**. (If you leave **Bin Range** blank, the procedure creates a set of bins that will not be as well-formed as the ones you can specify.)

2. Check **Labels** and click **New Worksheet Ply**.

3. Click **OK** to create the frequency distribution on a new worksheet.

Histogram

Input

Input Range: F1:F88

Bin Range: J1:J11

☑ Labels

Output options

○ Output Range:
● New Worksheet Ply:
○ New Workbook

☐ Pareto (sorted histogram)
☐ Cumulative Percentage
☐ Chart Output

[OK] [Cancel] [Help]

In the new worksheet:

4. Select row 1. Right-click row 1 and click the **Insert** shortcut menu. Repeat. (This creates two blank rows at the top of the worksheet.)

5. Enter a title for the frequency distribution in cell A1.

The ToolPak creates a frequency distribution that contains an improper bin labeled **More**. Correct this error as follows:

6. Manually add the frequency count of the **More** row to the count of the preceding bin. (This is unnecessary if the **More** count is 0, as it is in this Table 2.9 example.)

7. Click the worksheet row number for the **More** row (to select the entire worksheet row), right-click on the row, and click **Delete** in the shortcut menu that appears.

Open to the **STCDATA worksheet** and repeat steps 1 through 7 with rows 1 through 98. Then cut and paste the results from the two frequency distributions to create a table similar to Table 2.9.

The Relative Frequency, Percentage, or Cumulative Percentage Distribution

PHStat2 To create these other distributions, first use the *PHStat2* instructions in "The Frequency Distribution, Part II" to create a frequency distribution that contains a column of percentages and cumulative percentages. To create a column of relative frequencies, reformat the percentage column. Select the cells containing the percentages, right-click, and then select **Format Cells** from the shortcut menu. In the **Number** tab of the Format Cells dialog box, select **Number** as the **Category** and click **OK**.

In-Depth Excel To create these other distributions, modify a frequency distribution created using the *In-Depth Excel* instructions in "The Frequency Distribution, Part II" by adding a column for percentages (or relative frequencies) and a column for cumulative percentages. For example, open to the **FD_IG worksheet** of the **Chapter 2 workbook**.

This worksheet contains the frequency distribution for the intermediate government bond funds. To modify this worksheet to include percentage and cumulative percentage distributions:

1. Enter **Total** in cell **A14** and enter **=SUM(B4:B13)** in cell **B14**.

2. Enter **Percentage** in cell **C3** and **Cumulative Pctage** in cell **D3**.

3. Enter **=B4/$B$14** in cell **C4** and copy this formula down through all the rows of the frequency distribution.

4. Enter **=C4** in cell **D4**. Enter **=D4 + C5** in cell **D5** and copy this formula down through all the rows of the frequency distribution.

5. Select the cell range **C4:D13**, right-click, and click **Format Cells** in the shortcut menu.

6. In the **Number** tab of the Format Cells dialog box, select **Percentage** as the **Category** and click **OK**.

If you want a column of relative frequencies instead of percentages, change the cell **C4** column heading to **Rel. Frequencies**. Then select the cell range **C4:C13**, right-click, and click **Format Cells** in the shortcut menu. In the **Number** tab of the Format Cells dialog box, select **Number** as the **Category** and click **OK**.

Analysis ToolPak Use the preceding *In-Depth Excel* instructions to modify a frequency distribution created using the "The Frequency Distribution, Part II" instructions.

EG2.4 VISUALIZING CATEGORICAL DATA

The Bar Chart and the Pie Chart

PHStat2 Modify the Section EG2.2 *PHStat2* instructions for creating a summary table (page 74) to create a bar or pie chart. In step 3 of those instructions, check either **Bar Chart** and/or **Pie Chart** in addition to entering a **Title** and clicking **OK**.

In-Depth Excel Create a bar or pie chart from a summary table. For example, to create the Figure 2.2 bar chart on page 41 or the Figure 2.4 pie chart on page 42, open to the **SUMMARY_PIVOT worksheet** of the **Chapter 2 workbook** and:

1. Select cell range **A4:B7** (Begin your selection at cell B7 and not at cell A4, as you would normally do).

2. Click **Insert**. For a bar chart, click **Bar** in the **Charts group** and then select the first **2-D Bar** gallery choice (**Clustered Bar**). For a pie chart, click **Pie** in the **Charts group** and then select the first **2-D Pie** gallery choice (**Pie**).

3. Relocate the chart to a chart sheet and adjust the chart formatting by using the instructions in Appendix Section F.4.

For a pie chart, select **Layout →Data Labels → More Data Label Options**. In the Format Data Labels dialog box, click **Label Options** in the left pane. In the Label Options right pane, check **Category Name** and **Percentage** and clear the other check boxes. Click **Outside End** and then click **Close**.

For a bar chart, if the horizontal axis scale does not begin with 0, right-click the horizontal (value) axis and click **Format Axis** in the shortcut menu. In the Format Axis dialog box, click **Axis Options** in the left pane. In the Axis Options right pane, click the first **Fixed** option button (for Minimum) and enter **0** in its box. Click **Close**.

The Pareto Chart

PHStat2 Modify the Section EG2.2 *PHStat2* instructions for creating a summary table on page 74 to create a Pareto chart. In step 3 of those instructions, check **Pareto Chart** in addition to entering a **Title** and clicking **OK**.

In-Depth Excel To create a Pareto chart, modify the summary table that was originally created using the instructions in Section EG2.3. In the original table, first sort the table in order of decreasing frequencies and then add a column for cumulative percentage. Use the sorted, modified table to create the Pareto chart.

For example, to create the Figure 2.5 Pareto chart, open to the **ATMTable worksheet** of the **ATM Transactions workbook**. Begin by sorting the modified table by decreasing order of frequency:

1. Select row **11** (the Total row), right-click, and click **Hide** in the shortcut menu. (This prevents the total row from getting sorted.)

2. Select cell **B4** (the first frequency), right-click, and select **Sort → Sort Largest to Smallest**.

3. Select rows **10** and **12** (there is no row 11), right-click, and click **Unhide** in the shortcut menu.

Next, add a column for cumulative percentage:

4. Enter **Cumulative Pctage** in cell **D3**. Enter **=C4** in cell **D4**. Enter **=D4 + C5** in cell **D5** and copy this formula down through row 10.

5. Select the cell range **C4:D10**, right-click, and click **Format Cells** in the shortcut menu.

6. In the **Number** tab of the Format Cells dialog box, select **Percentage** as the **Category** and click **OK**.

Next, create the Pareto chart:

7. Select the cell range **A3:A10** and while holding down the **Ctrl** key also select the cell range **C3:D10**.

8. Select **Insert → Column** (in the Charts group) and select the first **2-D Column** gallery choice (**Clustered Column**).

9. Select **Format** (under **Chart Tools**). In the Current Selection group, select the entry for the cumulative percentage series from the drop-down list and then click **Format Selection**.

10. In the Format Data Series dialog box, click **Series Options** in the left pane and in the **Series Options** right pane, click **Secondary Axis**. Click **Close**.

11. With the cumulative percentage series still selected in the Current Selection group, select **Design → Change Chart Type**, and in the **Change Chart Type** gallery, select the fourth **Line** gallery choice (**Line with Markers**). Click **OK**.

Next, set the maximum value of the primary and secondary (left and right) *Y* axes scales to 100%. For each *Y* axis:

12. Right-click on the axis and click **Format Axis** in the shortcut menu.

13. In the Format Axis dialog box, click **Axis Options** in the left pane and in the **Axis Options** right pane, click the second **Fixed** option button (for Maximum) and enter **1** in its box. Click **Close**.

Relocate the chart to a chart sheet and adjust chart formatting by using the instructions in Appendix Section F.4.

When using a PivotTable as a summary table, table sorting is simpler: Right-click the cell that contains the first frequency (cell B5 in the sample worksheet) and select **Sort → Sort Largest to Smallest**. However, creating a Pareto chart from a PivotTable with additional columns for percentage and cumulative percentage is much more difficult than creating a chart from a simple summary table. The best workaround is to convert the PivotTable to a simple summary table by copying the category names and frequencies in the PivotTable, along with the additional columns, to an empty worksheet area.

The Side-by-Side Chart

PHStat2 Modify the Section EG2.2 *PHStat2* instructions for creating a contingency table on page 75 to create a side-by-side chart. In step 4 of those instructions, check **Side-by-Side Bar Chart** in addition to entering a **Title** and clicking **OK**.

In-Depth Excel Create a chart based on a contingency table to create a side-by-side chart. For example, to create the Figure 2.7 side-by-side bar chart on page 45, open to the **CONTINGENCY_PIVOT worksheet** of the **Chapter 2 workbook** and:

1. Select cell **A4** (or any other cell inside the PivotTable).

2. Select **Insert → Bar** and select the first **2-D Bar** gallery choice (**Clustered Bar**). Relocate the chart to a chart sheet and adjust the chart formatting by using the instructions in Appendix Section F.4, but with this exception: When you click **Legend**, select **Show Legend at Right**.

When creating a chart from a contingency table that is not a PivotTable, select the cell range of the contingency table, including row and column headings, but excluding the total row and total column, before selecting **Insert → Bar**.

Occasionally when you create a side-by-side chart, the row and column variables need to be swapped. If a Pivot-Table is the source for the chart, rearrange the PivotTable by making the row variable the column variable and vice versa. If the chart is not based on a PivotTable, right-click the chart and then click **Select Data** in the shortcut menu. In the Select Data Source dialog box, click **Switch Row/Column** and then click **OK**. (In Excel 2010, you can also use this second method for PivotTable-based charts.)

You may also need to rearrange the order of categories shown on the chart. To flip their positions for a chart based on a PivotTable, click the pull-down list for the categorical variable that needs to be rearranged and select **Sort A to Z**. In this example, after step 2, click the **Fees** pull-down list for the categorical variable that needs to be rearranged and select **Sort A to Z**. To rearrange the order of categories for a chart not based on a PivotTable, physically rearrange the worksheet columns that contain the data for the chart.

EG2.5 VISUALIZING NUMERICAL DATA

The Stem-and-Leaf Display

PHStat2 Use the **Stem-and-Leaf Display** procedure to create a stem-and-leaf display. For example, to create a stem-and-leaf display similar to Figure 2.8 on page 48, open to the **STCDATA worksheet** of the **Chapter 2 workbook**. Select **PHStat → Descriptive Statistics → Stem-and-Leaf Display**. In the procedure's dialog box (shown below):

1. Enter **F1:F98** as the **Variable Cell Range** and check **First cell contains label**.

2. Leave **Autocalculate stem unit** selected.

3. Enter a **Title** and click **OK**.

Because Minitab uses a truncation method and PHStat2 uses a rounding method, the leaves of the PHStat2 display differ slightly from Figure 2.8 (created using Minitab).

When creating other displays, use the **Set stem unit as** option sparingly and only if **Autocalculate stem unit** creates a display that has too few or too many stems. (Any stem unit you specify must be a power of 10.)

In-Depth Excel Manually construct the stems and leaves on a new worksheet to create a stem-and-leaf display. Use the **STEM_LEAF worksheet** of the **Chapter 2 workbook** as a guide to formatting your display.

The Histogram

PHStat2 Use the **Histogram & Polygons** procedure to create a histogram from unsummarized data. For example, to create the pair of histograms shown in Figure 2.10 on page 49, open to the **DATA worksheet** of the **Bond Funds workbook**. Select **PHStat → Descriptive Statistics → Histogram & Polygons**. In the procedure's dialog box (shown below):

1. Enter **F1:F185** as the **Variable Cell Range**, **J1:J11** as the **Bins Cell Range**, **K1:K10** as the **Midpoints Cell Range**, and check **First cell in each range contains label**.

2. Click **Multiple Groups - Stacked** and enter **B1:B185** as the **Grouping Variable Cell Range**. (In the DATA worksheet, the 2009 returns for both types of bond funds are stacked, or placed in a single column. The column B values allow PHStat2 to separate the returns for intermediate government funds from the returns for the short-term corporate funds.)

3. Enter a **Title**, check **Histogram**, and click **OK**.

The **Bins Cell Range** and the **Midpoints Cell Range** should appear in the same worksheet as the unsummarized data, as the DATA worksheet of the Bond Funds workbook illustrates. Because a first bin can never have a midpoint (because that bin does not have a lower boundary value defined), the procedure assigns the first midpoint to the second bin and uses "---" as the label for the first bin. Therefore, the **Midpoints Cell Range** you enter must be one cell smaller in size than the **Bins Cell Range**. Read "The Histogram: Follow-up" in the next column for an additional adjustment that you can apply to the histograms created.

In-Depth Excel Create a chart from a frequency distribution. For example, to create the Figure 2.10 pair of histograms on page 49, first use the Section EG2.4 "The Frequency Distribution, Part II" *In-Depth Excel* instructions on page 77.

Follow those instructions to create a pair of frequency distributions, one for the intermediate government bond funds, and the other for the short-term corporate bond funds, on separate worksheets. In each worksheet, add a column of midpoints by entering the column heading **Midpoints** in cell **C3**, '--- in cell **C4**, and starting in cell **C5**, the midpoints −7.5, −2.5, 2.5, 7.5, 12.5, 17.5, 22.5, 27.5, and 32.5. In each worksheet:

1. Select the cell range **B3:B13** (the cell range of the frequencies).
2. Select **Insert → Column** and select the first **2-D Column** gallery choice (**Clustered Column**).
3. Right-click the chart background and click **Select Data**.

In the Select Data Source dialog box:

4. Click **Edit** under the **Horizontal (Categories) Axis Labels** heading.
5. In the Axis Labels dialog box, enter the cell range *formula* in the form =*SheetName*!**C4:C13** (where *SheetName* is the name of the current worksheet) and then click **OK** to return to the Select Data Source dialog box.
6. Click **OK**.

In the chart:

7. Right-click inside a bar and click **Format Data Series** in the shortcut menu.

In the Format Data Series dialog box:

8. Click **Series Options** in the left pane. In the Series Options right pane, change the **Gap Width** slider to **No Gap**. Click **Close**.

Relocate the chart to a chart sheet and adjust the chart formatting by using the instructions in Appendix Section F.4. Read "The Histogram: Follow-up" on page for an additional adjustment that you can apply to the histograms created.

Analysis ToolPak Modify the Section EG2.3 Analysis ToolPak instructions for "The Frequency Distribution, Part II" on page 77 to create a histogram. In step 5 of those instructions, check **Chart Output** before clicking **OK**.

For example, to create the pair of histograms in Figure 2.10 on page 49, use the modified step 5 with both the

IGDATA and **STCDATA** worksheets of the **Chapter 2 workbook** (as discussed on page 77) to create a pair of worksheets that contain a frequency distribution and a histogram. Each histogram will have (the same) two formatting errors that you can correct:

To eliminate the gaps between bars:

1. Right-click inside one of the histogram bars and click **Format Data Series** in the shortcut menu that appears.
2. In the **Series Options pane** of the Format Data Series dialog box, move the **Gap Width** slider to **No Gap** and click **Close**.

To change the histogram bin labels:

1. Enter the column heading **Midpoints** in cell **C3** and enter '--- in cell **C4** (the first bin has no midpoint). Starting in cell **C5**, enter the midpoints −7.5, −2.5, 2.5, 7.5, 12.5, 17.5, 22.5, 27.5, and 32.5, in column C. (The midpoints will serve as the new bin labels in step 3.)
2. Right-click the chart background and click **Select Data**.
3. In the Select Data Source dialog box, click **Edit** under the **Horizontal (Categories) Axis Labels** heading. In the Axis Labels dialog box, enter the cell range *formula* in the form =*SheetName*!**C4:C13** as the **Axis label range** and click **OK**. Back in the Select Data Source dialog box, click **OK** to complete the task.

In step 3, substitute the name of the worksheet that contains the frequency distribution and histogram for *SheetName* and note that the cell range **C4:C13** does not include the column heading cell. Read the next section for an additional adjustment that you can apply to the histograms created.

The Histogram: Follow-up

Because the example used throughout "The Histogram" uses a technique that uses an extra bin (see "The Frequency Distribution, Part I" in Section EG2.4), the histogram created will have the extra, meaningless bin. If you would like to remove this extra bin, as was done for the histograms shown in Figure 2.10, right-click the histogram background and click **Select Data**. In the Select Data Source Data dialog box, first click **Edit** under the **Legend Entries (Series)** heading. In the Edit Series dialog box, edit the **Series values** cell range formula. Then click **Edit** under the **Horizontal (Categories) Axis Labels** heading. In the Axis Labels dialog box, edit the **Axis label range**. For the example used in the previous section, change the starting cell for the **Series values** cell range formula from B4 to B5 and change the starting cell for the **Axis label range** cell range formula from C4 to C5.

The Percentage Polygon

PHStat2 Modify the *PHStat2* instructions for creating a histogram on page 80 to create a percentage polygon. In step 3 of those instructions, click **Percentage Polygon** before clicking **OK**.

In-Depth Excel Create a chart based on a modified percentage distribution to create a percentage polygon. For example, to create the Figure 2.12 percentage polygons on page 50, open to the **CPD_IG worksheet** of the **Bond Funds workbook**. (This worksheet contains a frequency distribution for the intermediate government bond funds and includes columns for the percentages and cumulative percentages in column C and D.) Begin by modifying the distribution:

1. Enter the column heading **Midpoints** in cell **E3** and enter '--- in cell **E4** (the first bin has no midpoint). Starting in cell **E5**, enter −7.5, −2.5, 2.5, 7.5, 12.5, 17.5, 22.5, 27.5, and 32.5, in column E.

2. Select row 4 (the first bins row), right-click, and select **Insert** in the shortcut menu.

3. Select row 15 (the total row), right-click, and select **Insert** in the shortcut menu.

4. Enter 0 in cells **C4**, **D4** and **C15**.

5. Select the cell range **C3:C15**.

Next, create the chart:

6. Select **Insert → Line** and select the fourth **2-D Line** gallery choice (**Line with Markers**).

7. Right-click the chart and click **Select Data** in the shortcut menu.

In the Select Data Source dialog box:

8. Click **Edit** under the **Legend Entries (Series)** heading. In the Edit Series dialog box, enter the formula **="Intermediate Government"** for the Series name and click **OK**.

9. Click **Edit** under the **Horizontal (Categories) Axis Labels** heading. In the Axis Labels dialog box, enter the cell range formula **=CPD_IG!E4:E15** for the **Axis label range** and click **OK**.

10. Back in the Select Data Source dialog box, click **OK**.

Back in the chart sheet:

11. Right-click the vertical axis and click **Format Axis** in the shortcut menu.

12. In the Format Axis dialog box, click **Number** in left pane and then select **Percentage** from the **Category** list in the Number right pane. Enter **0** as the **Decimal places** and click **OK**.

Relocate the chart to a chart sheet and adjust the chart formatting by using the instructions in Appendix Section F.4.

Figure 2.12 on page 50 also contains the percentage polygon for the short-term corporate bond funds. To add this polygon to the chart just created, open to the **CPD_STC worksheet**. Repeat steps 1 through 5 to modify this distribution. Then open to the chart sheet that contains the intermediate government polygon. Select **Layout → Legend → Show Legend at Right**. Right-click the chart and click **Select Data** in the shortcut menu. In the Select Data Source

dialog box, click **Add**. In the Edit Series dialog box, enter the formula **="Short Term Corporate"** as the **Series name** and enter the cell range formula **=CPD_STC!C4:C15** as the **Series values**. Click **OK**. Back in the Select Data Source dialog box, click **OK**.

The Cumulative Percentage Polygon (Ogive)

PHStat2 Modify the *PHStat2* instructions for creating a histogram on page 80 to create a cumulative percentage polygon, In step 3 of those instructions, click **Cumulative Percentage Polygon (Ogive)** before clicking **OK**.

In-Depth Excel Create a cumulative percentage polygon by modifying the *In-Depth Excel* instructions for creating a percentage polygon. For example, to create the Figure 2.14 cumulative percentage polygons on page 52, use the instructions for creating percentage polygons, replacing steps 4 and 8 with the following:

4. Select the cell range **D3:D14**.

8. Click **Edit** under the **Horizontal (Categories) Axis Labels** heading. In the Axis Labels dialog box, enter the cell range formula **=CPD_IG!A4:A14** for the **Axis label range** and click **OK**.

Later, when adding the second polygon for the short-term corporate bond funds, enter the cell range formula **=CPD_STC!D4:D14** as the **Series values** in the Edit Series dialog box.

EG2.6 VISUALIZING TWO NUMERICAL VARIABLES
The Scatter Plot

PHStat2 Use the **Scatter Plot** procedure to create a scatter plot. For example, to create a scatter plot similar to the one shown in Figure 2.15 on page 55, open to the **DATA worksheet** of the **NBAValues workbook**. Select **PHStat2 → Descriptive Statistics → Scatter Plot**. In the procedure's dialog box (shown below):

1. Enter **C1:C31** as the **Y Variable Cell Range**.

2. Enter **B1:B31** as the **X Variable Cell Range**.

3. Check **First cells in each range contains label**.

4. Enter a **Title** and click **OK**.

You can also use the **Scatter Plot** output option of the **Simple Linear Regression** procedure to create a scatter plot. Scatter plots created using this alternative will contain a superimposed line like the one seen in Figure 2.15. (See the Excel Guide for Chapter 12 for the instructions for using the Simple Linear Regression procedure.)

In-Depth Excel Use a worksheet in which the column for the X variable data is to the left of the column for the Y variable data to create a scatter plot. (If the worksheet is arranged Y then X, cut and paste the Y variable column to the right of the X variable column.)

For example, to create a scatter plot similar to the one shown in Figure 2.15 on page 55, open to the **DATA worksheet** of the **NBAValues workbook** and:

1. Select the cell range **B1:C31**.
2. Select **Insert → Scatter** and select the first **Scatter** gallery choice (**Scatter with only Markers**).
3. Select **Layout → Trendline → Linear Trendline**.

Relocate the chart to a chart sheet and adjust the chart formatting by using the instructions in Appendix Section F.4.

The Time-Series Plot

In-Depth Excel Create a chart from a worksheet in which the column for the time variable data appears to the immediate left of the column for the numerical variable data. (Use cut and paste to rearrange columns, if necessary.)

For example, to create the Figure 2.16 time-series plot on page 56, open to the **DATA worksheet** of the **MovieGross workbook** and:

1. Select the cell range **A1:B15**.
2. Select **Insert → Scatter** and select the fourth **Scatter** gallery choice (**Scatter with Straight Lines and Markers**).

Relocate the chart to a chart sheet and adjust the chart formatting by using the instructions in Appendix Section F.4.

EG2.7 ORGANIZING MULTIDIMENSIONAL DATA

Multidimensional Contingency Tables

In-Depth Excel Use PivotTables to create multidimensional contingency tables. For example, to create the Figure 2.18 fund type, risk, and fees table on page 59, open to the **DATA worksheet** of the **Bond Funds workbook** and select **Insert → PivotTable**. In the Create PivotTable dialog box:

1. Click **Select a table or range** and enter **A1:I185** as the **Table/Range**.
2. Click **New Worksheet** and then click **OK**.

In the PivotTable Field List task pane (shown below):

3. Drag **Type** in the **Choose fields to add to report** box and drop it in the **Row Labels** box.
4. Drag **Risk** in the **Choose fields to add to report** box and drop it in the **Row Labels** box.
5. Drag **Fees** in the **Choose fields to add to report** box and drop it in the **Column Labels** box.
6. Drag **Fees** in the **Choose fields to add to report** box a second time and drop it in the **Σ Values** box. (This label changes to **Count of Fees**.)

In the PivotTable being created:

7. Click the **Fees** drop-down list in cell B3 and select **Sort Z to A** to rearrange the order of the "No" and "Yes" columns.
8. Right-click and then click **PivotTable Options** in the shortcut menu that appears.

In the PivotTable Options dialog box:

9. Click the **Layout & Format** tab.
10. Check **For empty cells, show** and enter **0** as its value. Leave all other settings unchanged.
11. Click the **Total & Filters** tab.
12. Check **Show grand totals for columns** and **Show grand totals for rows**.
13. Click **OK** to complete the table.

If you create a PivotTable from an **.xlsx** file in Excel 2007 or later, the default formatting of the PivotTable will differ from the formatting of the PivotTables shown in Section 2.7. Also, in step 7 you will always see **Column Labels** as the name of drop-down list and that drop-down list will appear in cell B3.

To display the cell values as percentages, as was done in Figures 2.20 and 2.21 on page 60, click **Count of Fees** in the PivotTable Field List task pane and then click **Value Field Settings** from the shortcut menu. In the Value Field Settings dialog box (shown below):

1. Click the **Show Values As** tab.

2. Select **% of Grand Total** from the **Show values as** drop-down list.

3. Click **OK**.

Adding Numerical Variables

In-Depth Excel Add a numerical variable to a PivotTable by dragging a numerical variable label from the **Choose fields to add to report** box to the Σ **Values** box and deleting the **Count of** *categorical variable* label (by dragging the label and dropping it anywhere outside the Σ **Values** box). To display something other than the sum of the numerical variable, click the **Sum of** *numerical variable* and then click **Value Field Settings** and make the appropriate entries in the Value Field Settings dialog box.

For example, to create the Figure 2.22 PivotTable of fund type, risk, and fees, showing averages of the 2009 return (see page 60) from the Figure 2.18 PivotTable, first create the Figure 2.18 PivotTable using steps 1 through 12 of the preceding section. Then continue with these steps:

13. Drag **Return 2009** in the **Choose fields to add to report** box and drop it in the Σ Values box. (This label changes to **Sum of Return 2009**.)

14. Drag **Count of Fees** in the Σ **Values** box and drop it anywhere outside that box.

15. Click **Sum of Return 2009** and click **Value Field Settings** from the shortcut menu.

In the Value Field Settings dialog box (shown below):

16. Click the **Summarize Values By** tab and select **Average** from the list. The label **Sum of Return 2009** changes to **Average of Return 2009**.

17. Click **OK**.

Adjust the cell formatting and decimal place display as required (see Appendix F).